D1715864

Post-Pandemic Human Resource Management

Key Concepts and Evidence-Backed
Philosophies to Help HR Professionals
Excel in Their Roles and Better Serve
Their Organizations

Betty Jimenez, PHR®, SPHR®

circumstances is the author responsible for any losses, direct or indirect, that are incurred as a result of the use of the information contained within this document, including, but not limited to, errors, omissions, or inaccuracies.

Table of Contents

Introduction

What next after COVID-19?

The world over, everyone is grappling with the effects of the pandemic. For organizations and individuals alike, the pandemic has been devastating. Lives and livelihoods were lost. What wasn't lost on us, however, is our resilience—the fabric of our being. No matter the adversity, we must pick up the pieces, pull together, and forge ahead.

The drastic changes occasioned by the pandemic put more pressure on human resource managers all over the world to have to rethink their roles and adjust to different policies and practices in the new work environment. Video conferences and email communication replaced in-person meetings. Companies didn't just adopt a remote working model, they were forced to and had to roll it out at an unprecedented scale and speed. The biggest challenge for human resource managers has been overseeing these changes while at the same time trying to ensure the dynamics of remote working don't hamper organizational goals and culture.

With the pandemic underpinning every strategic decision, employee well-being and health must also take center stage now more than ever. There's also the reality of laying off employees, especially in organizations whose financial forecasts have been bleak. Millions lost their jobs, leaving Human Resources (HR) managers with the difficult task of effecting job cuts while offering solace to the affected.

At a personal level, the pandemic had many people rethinking their personal goals and priorities in life, and their impact on the quality of life they desired going forward. This also occasioned voluntary exits from many workplaces. Beyond this, managers had to find ways of motivating and keeping the remaining employees engaged, productive, and committed.

Indeed, the remote working model has existed in many organizations for years. However, no one expected that it could be the new normal. Even so, no one anticipated the kind of difficulties we've experienced in accessing crucial support services for remote working employees, like hospitals and schools. By design, remote working models were meant to supplement the conventional office model and would mostly be sanctioned on an as-needed basis.

HR managers must work in haste with relevant departments, especially the Information Technology (IT) teams, to make this process efficiently flexible and productive. This means creating scalable solutions and procuring the equipment necessary to support the remote working models where they are rolled out en masse. Even more important is the need to ensure teams can still work together on projects remotely without interfering with the project quality and timelines.

Many companies have had to shift their perspective and rethink their approach to issues by looking at things from the employees' point of view. The fact that most people are working remotely and might keep doing so in the foreseeable future means that the emphasis is shifting towards replicating the enabling working environment in offices to individual homes. In line with employee health care needs, HR teams have to go above and beyond the standard duty of care often expected in the traditional work environment.

Companies that have in-house medical teams at work must still ensure that their teams get the support they need at all times, including their families, up to the extent allowable in their employment contracts. For COVID-related complications, they must also factor in the cost of testing and treatment not just for the employees but their families too.

What people do in their homes is not under the company's purview, but at the same time, companies must ensure their teams are comfortable enough in their homes to meet their deliverables. This is particularly important when it comes to marijuana usage. As more states legalize the use of marijuana, employers might struggle to implement relevant policies, especially since many people are working from home. In some cases, both local and state laws offer employees legal protections to use recreational marijuana off-duty. This particularly applies to those who need medical marijuana as part of a comprehensive treatment plan. Therefore, there's a need to update testing policies to accommodate the needs of such employees, both at home and within the office premises, where applicable.

The biggest challenge with marijuana use laws is compliance, as the applicable laws are not standardized across the country. While some states confer legal protections to employees, others might encourage employers to take stern action against recreational marijuana usage. There's a possibility of marijuana being legalized at the federal level in the near future, especially if current pressure on Congress is anything to go by. Until this happens, however, HR managers might continue struggling with the practicality of substance use laws, especially in remote working models where the company has no jurisdiction in the employee's home.

These challenges notwithstanding, employers must at least ensure access to the necessary healthcare facilities should their employees need them and, where possible, streamline access to support systems if they are ever needed.

At the management level, employers also need to ensure management teams have the necessary resources to execute their supervisory and administrative mandates. Organizational and other strategic meetings must still take place, albeit virtually. One key aspect that HR teams must also address is revising contingency measures to address the shortage of some specific skills.

It might have been unimaginable sometime ago but the reality of remote working being a permanent feature is imminent. This isn't just about the pandemic but also that many companies realize that, with the right changes, remote working offers an opportunity to give employees a wholesome and comfortable working experience. On the financial side, remote working means that companies don't need so much space, so they can save on their lease agreements and contracts.

Given that many companies were already figuring out the dynamics of remote working even before the pandemic, this trend will persist in the near future. The challenge for managers is figuring out how to streamline all processes and attain the desired productivity levels. HR managers must find ways of strengthening relationships between employees, teams, and other stakeholders within the corporate environment while at the same time adapting to evolving HR roles.

Chapter 1

Enhanced Customer Focus and Increased Business Agility

While the pandemic has resulted in noticeable changes in companies all over the world, there's no single department that has faced the brunt more than the human resource department. Given their oversight role, decisions affecting all the other departments eventually come down to HR. If we look at the disruptive impact of the pandemic, it's safe to say that the role of the human resources manager has pretty much become crisis control, since they have to make most of the difficult and often painful decisions, underlined by a pandemic that seems to have no end in sight.

As much as the global workforce is often encouraged to adapt to the demands of the new reality, HR teams have to go over and above everyone else, because more often, this is where the buck stops. Thus, real-time resilience, adaptability, and crisis management have been the backbone of HR through the pandemic and will be the foundation for progress post-pandemic.

Amidst the chaos of the pandemic, companies have had to make difficult decisions to stay afloat. In light of the organization's need and prospect for continuity, HR teams are tasked with handling benefits, engaging employees during the pandemic, compensation, and, where necessary, terminating contracts. It gets worse; with many people working from home, including HR teams, some of these decisions can take a personal toll on you.

It might be difficult to remain level-headed when you have to lay off people from your company, when you probably have people in your household who have suffered the same fate where they work, and you have shared in the strain of their personal challenges thereon. Thus, HR teams are, and might continue to face ethical dilemmas like these as long as the impact of the pandemic keeps biting.

We are facing uncertain times, and businesses must discuss a healthy transition protocol that will steer them safely through the turmoil. Even in the relatively stable business environment before the pandemic, the primary concern for HR teams revolved around the business culture, capabilities, and having the right mindset to lead employees and the company effectively in the right direction. These needs are heightened during difficult moments in the business cycle like the pandemic.

Market trends and customer preferences have never been static, so it would be foolhardy to suggest that the dynamic changes have been a result of the pandemic. What we can link to the pandemic, however, is the magnitude and speed with which the changes have taken place. The world over, people have been forced to make survival-level decisions on issues that they normally wouldn't need to, as the weight of the pandemic hit home.

While these changes are mostly unavoidable, considerable effort has been spent in managing them. The challenge for HR going forward is learning how to leverage these changes and turn them into valuable assets to steer the company through a difficult business environment.

Business Agility in a Pandemic

The socio-economic crisis arising from the COVID-19 pandemic has forced HR teams all over the world into a new model of crisis management, especially with many people working remotely. It's been more than a year down the line and most of the fears people had at the onset of the pandemic have since subsided. How are companies getting by? What are HR managers doing to get their teams working even though they cannot utilize the benefits of an in-person level of supervision? The short answer is business agility.

Remember that it's not just the companies and employees who are facing the challenges of the pandemic, customers are also feeling the pinch. With little room for investigation or research into customer responses and reactions, most of the changes effected in the workplace have been touch and go, hence the need for organizational agility.

Business agility is simply the company's strength in flexibility. This informs their ability to adapt and come up with creative solutions to enable them to evolve with the changing times or the demands of the new post-pandemic business environment. Agility makes it easier for the company to effect changes faster, timely respond to internal and external threats, and identify opportunities they can tap into.

"Success today requires the agility and drive to constantly rethink, reinvigorate, react, and reinvent"

~ Bill Gates

It's no secret that many companies have been pushed into unfamiliar territory since the pandemic. To overcome both the known and unknown challenges, HR teams must embrace agility, especially on financial and strategic matters. At the onset of the pandemic, the obvious choice for many organizations was to shield employees and the company, hence the drastic measures that were prevalent. However, now that the pandemic is a reality, there's no room for panic or drastic measures.

The pandemic has been a good learning experience for HR, and to map the way forward, there's a need for strategic approaches in managing customer expectations, looking after employee welfare, and planning for future economic uncertainty. These are the most important aspects of business agility that will lay the foundation for business agility through and after the pandemic.

Customer Expectations

When we talk about customer expectations, the question for HR is how to ensure the business caters to customer demands. Seeing that customers were also forced into survival mode, their demands and expectations have evolved in line with their immediate needs. Agile HR teams must restructure their operational models and resources to address these changes accordingly. Note that this also creates room for new opportunities which can be tapped into by the competition or new entrants in the industry. The crux, really, is on how fast HR and the company in general can adapt.

There has never been a better time to nurture customer relationships than this. Assuming that the worst comes to pass and you must cease operation for some time, be honest with your customers. Transparency can go a long way in strengthening your relationships with them. This is good for your brand reputation and might be the ace up your sleeve as you rebuild once the pandemic is over.

Employee Welfare

The wait-and-see approach is now outdated. Everyone has learned tough lessons and it's time to move on. To meet the first agility goal (customer expectations), you must ensure your employees are on the same page. This goes over and above employee motivation.

The pandemic had many people reevaluating their importance and value to their employers. A lot of people quit their jobs. They denied employers crucial skilled labor because they didn't feel valued enough. Some didn't think the companies cared for their mental health, well-being, and other personal concerns.

As long as your teams feel undervalued, you'll struggle to meet customer needs in a rapidly evolving business environment. Your employee turnover might also be higher, further exacerbating the problem of staffing in a market where skilled labor might be difficult to come by. The solution here is to restructure your team dynamics. Consider a new approach that revolves around change and crisis management. It could be as simple as clear responsibilities and delegation of duties, or as difficult as restructuring the entire workforce afresh.

The most important thing is to ensure that you have the right internal structures and processes to support the changes. Do you have COVID-19 protocols, policies, and management strategies in place? Are your remote working policies favorable to your employees? What if remote working is not feasible for your operation, for example, in retail and production centers? What assurances do your employees have on their safety as they carry out their mandate?

Economic Uncertainty

The unfortunate thing about the economy is that you cannot control it. A growth mindset, however, can help your teams navigate difficult moments. With this mindset, failure isn't a finality. Your teams learn to see failure as an important part of the growth process, learn from it, and make huge progressive strides into the future.

Failure was the undertone for many organizations during the pandemic. There was always that possibility that failure was imminent. Some companies succumbed to that fate, others forged on, faced the difficulties, and are still in operation today. The entertainment, hospitality, travel, and allied industries are some of the hardest hit in terms of financial adversity. Given the number of unknowns around COVID-19, it's almost impossible to aptly predict what happens next for these industries. We've had governments reopening their economies only to close them a few weeks later citing rising cases of new infections, reinfections, and fatalities.

Of course, a growth mindset alone won't get you across the line. Other factors like sound financial backing also come into play. Whether the company is able to finance operations during and after the pandemic might be beyond the purview of HR depending on the business structure. What you can do, however, is to align your teams in a manner that if your financial position allows, they have the mettle to weather the challenges of economic uncertainty.

Role of Agility in HR

Success in the post-pandemic corporate world will come down to collaboration and agility. This is because of the transformative impact of business agility, which will be necessary to bridge the gap between the pandemic-driven remote working models and getting back to a semblance of normalcy.

In post-pandemic HR, there's a need for adaptability and evolution both in the people and processes to support the organizational strategies. The duty of HR, therefore, is to push for better engagement and employee retention given that a lot of people's minds have shifted since the pandemic in terms of their role and importance in the corporate circle.

Traditionally, the role of HR is centered around the workforce. This means that HR is not directly associated with delivering value to customers. As the world evolves post-pandemic, it's important to reinvent HR in a manner that aligns with the company's need for customer satisfaction. HR must pay more attention to evolving business practices and technologies to enable them to become more responsive to both the needs of customers and the organization.

In this regard, it becomes easier for HR to identify issues affecting customers that can be addressed at the employee level, put measures in place to reduce the turnaround time for implementing appropriate responses, and, finally, institute analytical measures to help in mitigating successful programs. While other departments rely on technical solutions like Scrum for agility, HR doesn't need to. HR is practically not a technical function of the organization, so instead, they can adapt agile principles to immediate needs instead of going the technical way. Here are some approaches that highlight how to go about this:

Defined Agility Journey

When it comes to agility, every company has a unique needs system that works for them. Some concepts might cut across an industry, but once you take a microscopic view, you'll realize that every company is unique. Your challenges, as much as your ideal solutions, will come down to the customer profile you serve, your strategies, the skill composition within your workforce, and so on.

If you are to succeed in implementing agile practices, your strategies must be unique to your organization's needs. While it is important to study the market to get a feeling of your position in the industry, you cannot implement anything within the industry. You can only change things within your organization and align with the prevailing conditions in the industry. Define your company's agility needs in terms of the people, processes, and technology relevant to your organizational needs and objectives. Once you do that, it becomes easier to plan the way forward.

Strategic Product or Service Management

Whether you are in the product or service industry, you need a strategic management approach to refine your agility culture. This information gives you better insight into the kind of challenges you face at the organizational level, and how to create cost-effective solutions. The end game is to ensure that your customers always get the best quality at all times.

Customer needs, tastes, and preferences are always dynamic. Since the pandemic, however, the rate and magnitude of change have been quite unpredictable, as consumer needs shift to self-preservation. Unfortunately, the kind of disarray in consumer markets is further exacerbated by the fact that your employees are also going through upheavals in different aspects of their lives.

As much as you must try to be responsive to customer needs, you cannot skimp on value along the supply chain. One thing we learned from the uncertainties of the pandemic is that things can change rapidly, and to mitigate the changes, your company must be flexible in its approach to delivering value to customers. With efficient strategic management protocols, you can anticipate both internal and industry-wide changes, take the necessary steps, and ensure your customers get value.

In retrospect, uncertainty and the rapid changes in the business environment should give you a lot to think about. For example, it would be foolish to ignore the impact of changing customer expectations under the guise of pandemic-driven demands. The impact of the pandemic on your customers is not temporary. Customers are making changes to improve their lives or stay afloat, just as much as you have done as a business so far.

The dynamic changes notwithstanding, customers will always seek value from the market. Value can be delivered in many ways, including the addition of features or even offering them more variety to choose from. Apart from that, the modern customer's concept of value is more wholesome and goes beyond the value offered in product or service delivery. Customers also seek value in terms of the environmental and social impact of your business. They need to see that you don't just care about their money.

On your part, you can do so much to empower your employees so that they can deliver as per the customer's requirements. Everything we thought we knew about a modern workplace or workforce has been thrown out by the pandemic. The attention has shifted to HR to make sure that employees are comfortable whether they are working remotely or from your office.

Redirect your attention to improving the people processes, workplace practices, employee engagement, and company culture. One of your priorities after the pandemic will be to ensure you don't suffer a high employee turnover. Like your customers, employees also need value from their employer. This creates more pressure on HR to create an enabling business culture.

Running an agile operation in the post-pandemic business world means leveraging the best of technology in HR. There's so much to work with from software solutions to data analytics. All this is meant to help you build an adaptive, productive, and robust work environment that helps you bring out the best in your team.

Integrating agility into HR is primarily a leadership role; it's one that will lay the foundation for organizational growth and provide clear direction through uncertain times, and into an uncertain future. Thus, in your oversight HR role, you must stay connected and in touch with all changes taking place throughout the company. Everything from reshuffling employees across departments, adopting and implementing new technologies, and rethinking business strategies to meet new business targets should be at your fingertips. Your prerogative is to leverage efficiency and productivity to drive business growth.

Chapter 2

Lack of Agility

HR is traditionally a rigid department, shrouded in stringent standards, protocols, and controls. With this strict nature, implementing agility in HR has always been a struggle for many organizations, even though other departments have consistently realized good returns following that approach. HR was never built for agility and this has made the department lag behind.

The pandemic exacerbated almost all challenges that each department in an organization had been struggling with. The rigid nature of HR often made it difficult to implement drastic measures given the inability to respond or move faster. Before any action is implemented in HR, there usually are many approval levels to overcome, which only makes things worse. Now in a corporate environment where many people are working remotely, such drawbacks only create more bottlenecks to an HR practice that is already strained on all fronts.

A crisis situation like the pandemic, for example, demands data collection and rapid responses to address emerging concerns and issues affecting employees, both at home and in the workplace. It's impossible to achieve this with the traditional structure of HR, citing the slow pace of processes involved. With this in mind, therefore, it makes sense to reorganize HR towards an agile future.

Going forward, the lack of agility in HR will pose a lot of challenges to restructuring and reprioritizing organizational goals and objectives. This is why it's important for HR to address the issue of agility during this period where people are largely working from home. By integrating agile practices into HR, it becomes easier to test different strategies and phased implementation over time. Eventually, the goal is to welcome HR into an era of process automation and subsequently improve response times in crisis management.

Every department in an organization faces challenges from time to time. While challenges might create moments of chaos, they also act as unlikely motivators to learn and improve skills and abilities. Since the pandemic, HR departments have faced a lot of challenges. Overcoming them or, at the very least, attempting to solve them has helped many organizations become better at managing crisis situations.

In the absence of agility, HR departments might have succeeded at creating and implementing standards and processes that spur control and executing instructions. However, what's missing, which can be achieved with agility, is the need to shift HR's focus and mission to championing and improving agility throughout the company. This can only be achieved by pushing for radical changes that introduce collaboration, innovation, and adaptability which directly affect the speed of implementation.

We must also note that these are crucial points that have been at the core of many successful business models implemented during the pandemic and will continue to inspire organizational growth post-pandemic. Remember that the whole point of agility is on collaborative processes that allow gradual and measurable solutions to emerging problems. The gradual aspect of agility enables HR to experiment, test, and implement ideas faster by eliminating procedural bottlenecks that had existed earlier.

If implemented properly, agility in HR will enable your department to realize efficient implementation, innovation, and better performance. The crux of this process is that it moves HR from a culture of a stringent hierarchical approach to a collaborative, innovative, and feedback-oriented system, which eventually bodes well for people management and leadership.

All these are important, especially in a pandemic where attention is shifting from organizational objectives, to how organizations can create a wholesome and healthy working environment that enables employees to deliver and meet organizational objectives without the need for direct supervision or other definitively rigid structures.

Agility, after all, is about engagement and initiatives that support and empower your team.

What Agility Means to HR

Having mentioned the need for rapid change implementation amidst a pandemic, and the need to improve organizational focus, it's important to understand how this aligns with HR's approach to management. In a way, the pandemic forced HR's hands towards agility, probably faster than would have been anticipated. This is true because the pandemic highlighted the need for rapid adjustment to unpredictable circumstances across all departments.

Through agility, HR is able to conduct their support roles across all departments and, at the same time, offer reliable solutions throughout the organization. Over time, our thought processes and approaches to organizational problems and solutions will be influenced by the pandemic. This means that everything from strategic business goals to operations will be affected.

With the traditional business model already disrupted by remote working models, we can expect remote employee monitoring, teleworking, and more complex organizational structures in the future. These factors can, and will, reshape HR's approach to people management. Chances are high that many organizations will have to rethink staffing, with more looking towards contract or contingent employees over full-time employees, primarily as a cost-cutting solution.

By adopting agile processes, HR and the organization at large will be in a better position to handle most of the challenges facing modern businesses, such as low employee engagement, identifying and mentoring leadership at different organizational levels, managing a workforce whose demands and perspectives of the corporate environment is largely influenced by personal pandemic experiences, challenges with technological integration, and, more importantly, talent recruitment and management.

Through agile practices, organizations are in a better position to address their immediate needs, while at the same time balancing them against those of the dynamic employment landscape. For HR, there has never been a better time to move from theory to practice. The transition from traditional HR to agile HR will particularly cull the reliance on organizational hierarchy in decision making. One way to achieve this is to move away from strict job titles and role identities in favor of team selection based on individual talent and collaborative skills. This should deliver flexibility and transparency throughout the company.

Another challenge facing HR right now which can be addressed with agile practices is compensation. If your company has an equitable, fair compensation plan, you will find it easier to navigate the job market in the future. One notable result of the pandemic is that the global talent pool is not the same. Skill gaps have gotten thinner with more companies competing for the best talent in the market. To remain competitive, HR must constantly assess and review compensation structures, benefits, and pay packages in line with the market rates.

Since remote working will be here for a while, the decision-making approach must also change. Agility is about consistent engagement, facilitation, and feedback loops. HR can learn from blockchain technology and decentralize decision making. Empower employees to take responsibility and ownership of their input, make crucial decisions, and find lessons in mistakes. Encourage teams to self-assess through retrospective meetings where they can discuss and review completed projects. The purpose of such meetings is to gather insight, discuss challenges experienced, how they impeded progress, and how to mitigate them going forward. This is one of the best ways of improving decision-making processes throughout the organization, by having the people who are directly involved in processes taking center stage.

Finally, the foundation of agility is continuous learning and improvement. It might take time to fully transition your team into agile HR post-pandemic, but the investment will be worth every penny. There will be bumps along the way, but that's consistent with every learning curve.

Try different strategies, and adjust accordingly until you identify processes that are suitable to your organization's culture and needs. Ultimately, you will be better placed to understand your employees, and by addressing their needs, you can look forward to better engagement and a happy workforce.

The Hybrid Office

In March 2020, most workers were sent home abruptly, kickstarting what no one realized at the time, would be the new normal for more than a year. Working from home wasn't always going to be the most ideal solution, but we were facing a crisis on all fronts and it was the feasible option. Over time, the need for a hybrid office became more apparent and is one of the key considerations that HR must look into.

A hybrid workplace is basically a setup that allows employees the flexibility of working in whichever location they feel comfortable and most productive. This means that they can either work from home, the office, or both. The focus is on productivity, support, and flexibility.

Even though many people are coming across it for the first time, the concept of a hybrid office is not a new one. It has been around for a long time; it's rarely an option that many people or companies consider. In the traditional hybrid workplace, employees would have to outline their office days and remote working days in advance. This is different from the current hybrid workplace where you choose what works for you at that moment. Thus, you can wake up in the morning and start working from home, and once you feel the environment is no longer conducive for your productivity, you can either go to the park or the office.

One thing we can anticipate about the model hybrid office during and after the pandemic is that employees will enjoy more flexibility and choices. This comes from the fact that HR is inclined to pay more attention to employee needs. For a long time, productivity has always been the priority in HR without much attention to stimuli within the employee's environment that might affect their well-being. This changed during the pandemic as more emphasis was placed on making sure that employees are within the right frame of mind to carry out their mandate effectively.

In many industries, a lot of jobs might assume the remote working model permanently which bodes well with the push for more hybrid workspaces. Remote working is already the norm for many employees, so it's up to employers to weigh the pros and cons against productivity and overall employee engagement to determine whether to stick with the plan or resume in-office working. However, a more practical approach would be to implement hybrid working spaces and encourage more employees to come on board.

Indeed, the infrastructure for hybrid workspaces has always been there which means that employers should not encounter a lot of resistance at full implementation. If anything, many employees who often complained about not having enough time to participate in the lives of their loved ones can now enjoy the best of both worlds.

HR must now consider how to implement different software and tech solutions to ensure that whichever option employees choose, productivity and efficiency will not suffer. There are a lot of reasons why many people are optimistic about the hybrid model. One of the most important is the fact that the employee enjoys complete autonomy in the design of their office, especially the home office.

Most office spaces can be so boring, that they suck the life out of you each time you walk into the building. With the hybrid office, you can personalize your space whichever way you want without worrying about your colleagues being offended or taking an unnecessary interest in your workspace. Once you model your office according to your personality, you might realize that it becomes easier to focus on your work and meet deliverables with ease.

As much of the attention will shift to the home office or whichever remote working space you choose, let's not forget that the multi-use offices will still remain available, including most services and solutions that employers offer to streamline the working process. Therefore, while the traditional concept of a hybrid workspace might have evolved, you might still need to check in with HR from time to time if you wish to work from the office instead of at home. This is also important so that you can avoid being in an overcrowded office, just in case other employees choose to come to the office too.

The hybrid office model might also push HR to redesign the work week, and instead of the usual 9-5 Monday to Friday, we could switch to a system where employees split their week and work maybe three days at home, two in the office, and have the remaining two days off. Whichever solution your company chooses, the most important thing is to find the right balance that enables your teams to collaborate seamlessly regardless of their location, and still uphold the organization's goals and culture.

While employees will practically be in charge of their remote working stations at home, HR must be in control of redesigning the office landscape for everyone. To ensure that everyone at the office gets the support needed for a productive experience, HR must ensure the office is redesigned for collaboration. This means a shift from the individualized workspaces to a cozier structure that accommodates employee engagement.

Of course, this doesn't mean that individual workstations will be gone forever. The redesign should accommodate all employees, including those who simply want some peace and quiet to focus on their work. While remote working is widely lauded for changing the way we work, we must also be cognizant of the fact that all homes are not perfect for work. Some people have roommates, children, insufficient space, or unstable bandwidth. With these concerns, you'd expect that employees in such situations would prefer to work from the office, hence the need to make the office situation reliable for such cases.

Employee Engagement

One of the reasons why remote working had never gained so much traction before the pandemic was the challenge of employee engagement. For clarity, remote working has been around for many years, and many companies had been mulling how to implement it effectively in their operations and still achieve the desired levels of efficiency on productivity. Today, it is the new normal, and all companies, including those who had never considered it one bit, must beat the race against time to implement it with all the proper safeguards in place.

Granted, remote working has been great for many companies so far. The usual costs to keep offices running, like cleaning, electricity, internet, and water bills have gone down significantly. For the most part, employees working remotely are happier and more productive in the absence of rigid structures. Most of the stress factors that often hamper employee productivity in the office are not around anymore, so it's in the best interest of employers to keep improving remote working models or refine them to suit the demands of their business operations.

To ensure that employees keep delivering their best performance, employers must now address the issue of employee engagement and, while at it, how to keep the company culture alive. It doesn't matter where your employees are working from, it's your obligation to keep them engaged and aligned with the company culture.

You need to understand how employee engagement ties into remote work and your company culture. Remote working will be here for a long time, and might even be fully implemented by many organizations. With that in mind, you should address the pain points reported by your employees. Find out how it's working for them and what they think could use some improvement.

Engagement for employees who are working remotely poses a new challenge for employers. You have to do more than just provide good salaries and flexible working hours. People need to see and feel that you are genuine in your actions and intentions. Communication platforms like Slack and Zoom enjoyed significant growth during the pandemic as more employers tapped into their potential to streamline business processes. These platforms offer more than just business connectivity. You can also use them to create awareness in the organization.

A lot of people have missed the social interaction aspect of working together in an office since the pandemic and subsequent lockdowns were announced. Despite all the benefits of remote working, loneliness creeps in when you can't interact with people like you used to, and this can wear down even the best and most resilient of employees.

You can still leverage the power of platforms like Zoom for virtual meet-ups and team-building activities. If all you ever do online is work, it gets boring after a while, and people start looking for creative ways to avoid those interactions. Go beyond the meetings, create social hours where people can just come online and talk about anything else but work. Over time, people will look forward to these moments.

Don't just tell employees that you care for them, show them you do. There are many ways to go about this, and since most people are working from home, more room for flexibility in solutions. Where possible, encourage your employees to work with their team leaders or supervisors to define their own working schedules. The dynamics of individual homes are not the same, so it might be unfair to demand that everyone works 9-5 from their homes. Some people might be comfortable starting in the afternoon, others later in the evening.

Apart from giving them the freedom to choose flexible hours, you can also talk to them about emotional and mental health, how to manage their workload to avoid burnout, and how they are handling things like personal hobbies, family life, and so on. Even as you do this, remember there's a thin line between showing concern and prying too deep into their personal lives, so be sure to respect their boundaries.

Finally, how you communicate with your employees can make a big difference during this difficult time. This is particularly important on matters they raised. Let them know when you plan to act on something, or if you don't intend to do so, and with reasons. You might not be able to address all their needs at the same time, so give them a plan for anything you intend to handle in the future. These are some simple things that mean so much to employees, and make them feel valued, engaged, and happy to work for you.

Chapter 3

Increased Use of Analytics

Life as we know it will never be the same after the pandemic. One thing that has been evident in HR is the need to reinvent processes, talent management, communication, engagement, rewards, performance measures, and so on. These are crucial things in creating an enabling work environment. Companies always track employees. It's the only way they can gather sufficient data to support the factors mentioned above. Without these, it would be difficult to assess and authenticate remuneration packages and benefits for different employees.

Since HR is unable to enjoy in-person supervision and connections with the prevalence of remote working models, it's becoming difficult to implement the measures above and track employee performance. The fact that employers are struggling to track employees means that there's a lot of room for reinvention. Indeed, it's always in the best interest of employers to not only track what their employees are up to on company resources, but also to control it.

The phrase *trust, but verify,* borrowed from a Russian proverb and gained popularity during the Reagan Administration, is widely used in the corporate world and for a good reason. Blind trust can leave you exposed in the corporate world. Employers can extend their trust to employees as a show of good faith. However, tracking and control help them ensure that their trust is not abused, and all prudent measures are exercised at all times.

Companies have used employee monitoring software solutions in the past. However, as remote working makes it difficult to actively supervise their teams, more companies will implement these solutions in the future. While employers might be concerned about what employees do on company time whether in their offices or their remote stations, this isn't really their biggest concern. Post-pandemic, companies are mainly worried about the availability of crucial skills.

In light of the challenges arising from the pandemic, some of the most sought-after skills include leadership, creativity, problem solving, technical business skills, and adaptability. Possessing these skills makes a candidate a valuable asset to any organization, especially when we consider the kind of dynamic changes that companies must implement in the new business environment post-pandemic.

Tracking employees is one thing. There's so much valuable data obtained in those processes. The challenge for HR is what to do with that data. Your understanding and interpretation of that data can make a big difference in addressing immediate staffing concerns. One of the emerging trends in HR during the pandemic is the fact that crisis management has become a regular point of concern. In the push to reboot economies worldwide, there's a need for HR to start implementing people analytics, not just in meeting deliverables, but also to help improve productivity by following agile practices.

Innovative thinking in the new corporate environment must be supported by data-driven decision making. Other departments have used data analytics in the past to fruition and realized great results. It's time for HR to implement the same too, not just for crisis management around the pandemic, but to chart the way forward for the future.

How do you make sure targets are met as people work remotely? How can you keep people motivated and morale high in diverse remote working locations? By merging data analytics with HR, you should be in a better position to provide all the resources to support your teams, keep them focused on their deliverables, plan ahead, and measure the impact of the data-driven solutions.

Data analytics also offers an opportunity for HR to assess collaboration, productivity, and, while at it, ensure that employees do not suffer burnout from wherever they are. This will also make it easier to get tangible information on the impact of working from home on employee well-being.

Some of the approaches that companies have used in the past include monitoring employee communication through internal networks, employee chats and emails, tracking activity on computers, and virtual attendance registers. Most of these programs, when used with the right combination of solutions, can do more than just track productivity. They can also help you understand experiences.

In retrospect, employee tracking and monitoring are not new to HR. What we'll see after the pandemic is an accelerated emerging trend of widespread tracking and monitoring, not just at work, but also remotely. Apart from performance, HR will also be interested in overall safety and employee health data and following the best data protection practices to ensure that people analytics is responsibly and appropriately implemented.

Understanding People Analytics

People analytics, also known as talent analytics, is an elaborate HR function for gathering, analyzing, and reporting employee data. People analytics is one of the crucial aspects of integrating technology into HR practices that have largely been traditional and analog at best for many years. With people working from home, it is an important process that gives you access to a wide range of metrics on employee and business performance, which will go a long way in decision making.

Through and after the pandemic, calls for HR to evolve into a strategic function instead of an operational function will increase, as more companies grapple with the challenge of staying in control, or at the very least, maintaining some form of control over employee interaction as they work in different remote locations. The only way for employers to achieve this is by collecting and analyzing data on their teams.

People analytics takes HR into a deep data dive to understand functions, people processes, strengths, weaknesses, and how to identify opportunities. HR can leverage such information to identify growth opportunities at the individual level and, in the process, realize sustainable business success in the long run.

Access to such information brings a different dynamic to talent decisions like the need for training and redeployment across departments. Eventually, this can also help the company cut down on recruitment costs that would have otherwise been spent on external hiring, by finding and training the right individuals internally and preparing them for specific roles.

One good thing about people analytics is that you gain historical data on an employee, which is quite an invaluable asset for evaluating performance management over the years. Similar to other forms of business analytics, people analytics also leans more towards predictive analytics. This means that apart from learning about an employee, HR is in a good position to predict the actions or decisions of the employee based on historical data. This also gives HR the advantage of being well-prepared for dynamic changes in the company as a result of unavoidable circumstances like the pandemic.

For a long time, HR has always been reactive on talent decisions. With people analytics, however, HR assumes a more proactive role using complex data science and machine learning techniques to study and understand performance and employee behavior. People analytics also takes away the challenge of people management through gut feelings or instinct. In many organizations, people follow procedures and processes simply because that's how it's always been done. While it's a good thing to identify, align with the company's culture, the world around the company keeps evolving, and from time to time, it makes sense to step out of your comfort zone and try something new. This is where people analytics comes in.

Apart from that, HR has for a long time lagged behind other data-oriented departments like finance and marketing in terms of measuring performance in quantifiable metrics. This doesn't have to be the case anymore, with people analytics. HR can now evolve from a descriptive function to a data-driven and intricately analytical function.

As much as we can look forward to an employment environment where HR has more data and statistics on employee performance and can make better decisions, we cannot discount the importance of value-based decisions. Data from people analytics will improve the current HR processes, instead of replacing them. Before making a decision, it's important to consider and measure its possible tradeoffs and repercussions. This is what HR gets from people analytics. The onus now shifts to HR to establish a framework for what's acceptable and what's not. Thus, before implementing people analytics in your operations, make sure your current processes are refined and streamlined accordingly because analytics can only improve an efficient system.

Planning for Success

Even before businesses all over the world started rethinking their strategic approaches to management and operations, many companies were already implementing people analytics. This was informed by the need for a better understanding of a wide range of data-driven talent-based decisions. From this experience, it was only a matter of time before data analytics would become the focal point in human capital management. In this case, HR is looking to improve not just hiring decisions, but employee engagement, retention and compensation. It's safe to say that people analytics will usher HR into an amazing future post-pandemic.

As we emerge from the challenges caused by the pandemic, companies that embrace and successfully implement people analytics in their operations can anticipate exponential growth in all aspects of talent acquisition and management. While data analytics has been implemented in other departments, it is an emerging trend in HR, which means that there's more room and need for further investment.

Even though there's a lot of optimism around implementing people analytics, we cannot ignore the fact that HR will face several challenges as a result of the drastic changes to the workplace dynamics as a result of the pandemic. It is important, therefore, to review how the analytical approaches and solutions can evolve alongside business and employee needs. To understand this, we will consider how the role of HR has evolved by assessing talent management and employee well-being management.

Talent Management

Data analytics in HR was largely used to match people with the right skills to different roles in the organization. Staffing, as a key HR function, was largely informed by the prevailing state of the economy, which includes anything from the level of unemployment to inflation rates.

Driven by economics, talent acquisition and retention was highly competitive, not just across departments, but also within industries. As a result, many employers started using people analytics to refine their hiring and employee retention approaches. This also made it easier for HR departments to identify the best talent by considering among other things, whether they were a fit for the organization's culture.

Once the right personnel were in the company, the next hurdle for HR was managing employee turnover rates. The idea here was to understand employee engagement to a point where the company was in a better position to assess the needs of key employees. This way, the company can consider amicable solutions that can help them retain such employees before they serve a notice.

Eventually, innovative pressure pushed companies to delve deeper into people analytics and understand the dynamics of project accomplishment. How are teams going about their projects? Which teams have the best collaborative synchrony? How are brilliant or breakthrough ideas being conceived within teams? With this implementation, HR doesn't just get to understand people, they also understand people processes.

Employee Well-Being Management

At the moment, it's almost impossible to predict with certainty how the workplace will evolve after the pandemic. What we know, for a fact, is that HR will face new challenges and must rise to their demands accordingly. On talent management and employee well-being, HR must assess different approaches to find out which ones are effective, where, how, and their impact on the organization in general.

With the right implementation, people analytics can help improve employee well-being in different ways. One of the immediate results of data analysis is to help HR identify programs and benefits that have received the fastest or highest uptake amongst employees in terms of managing mental health.

More people are suffering from anxiety today than before the pandemic. Worry and uncertainty, job security, and personal concerns have also contributed to this problem. While social distancing has been of great help in preventing the spread of the virus, the isolation aspect disrupted many social constructs, pushing a lot of people into depression. Those who were used to working in close contact with their teammates had to contend with working alone in their homes. As long as an employee's state of mental health is at stake, their productivity will soon follow suit.

People management isn't just about monitoring their performance and other metrics. In terms of well-being, it's also about how you address their challenges during and after the coronavirus crisis. It's about the support systems you put in place right now to ensure that going forward you can mitigate well-being concerns and offer wholesome relatable solutions. This will not just improve the morale and productivity of your employees but will also make it easier for you to attract and retain the best talent groups in the market.

In the section above, we mentioned the need for HR to understand people processes. From this knowledge, you can forge stronger connections between teams, especially those that are working remotely. It will be of great help to understand the dynamics of team member interactions in remote settings. Together with team leaders and managers, you can come up with standards and guidelines for team interactions going forward.

The next phase is finding out how to motivate, empower, and champion collaborative strategies amongst remote workers. These are prerequisites for successful reintegration into whatever working arrangements you will implement after the pandemic. One way of going about this is to consider how the challenges that employees face while working remotely affect their productivity and the kind of challenges that made them think outside the box and come up with creative solutions.

For better insight, you can also compare the performance of teams before and after the pandemic on the same tasks. For example, there's cause for further investigation if the performance of two teams before the pandemic was consistent but this changed during or after the pandemic. That can give you good insight into how each team was affected. Lessons from how the best performing team has sustained their performance throughout can also guide you on how to support the struggling teams.

Before implementing people analytics solutions in your business, you need clear guidelines on desired outcomes, possible scenarios, and how to mitigate implementation challenges when they arise. This gives you the right framework for design, execution, and evaluation.

Chapter 4

Ethical Leadership Aligned Safety

HELP EACH OTHER!

For a long time, there has been pressure on HR to evolve and adapt employee-centric values and policies. The pandemic only succeeded at making this need more apparent and urgent. Before the pandemic, HR policies mostly revolved around compliance, cost-effectiveness, and standardization, with a bit of supporting integration from IT here and there. This largely points to a productivity-based approach with little regard for employee well-being.

Going forward, employee safety, mental health, and well-being demand that HR adopt ethical approaches to reinvent core processes. People-centric practices will influence all decisions including talent acquisition, development, and management. Thus, the pandemic accelerated the need for HR to take more interest in the moral concerns of society.

To be honest, we cannot aptly predict the direction or speed of change going forward. As much as people are being encouraged to get vaccinated, we still have cases of new infections, severe ones, and even fatal cases. From this point of view, the safest bet for HR in all possible solutions is to assume that the traditional workplace is unsafe. With this in mind, it's easier to empathize and understand the plight of employees who are unwilling to return to work right away. Remember that the welfare and well-being of your employees are of utmost importance going forward.

By factoring in these concerns, you also take a closer look at the concept of a toxic working environment. When they do, people will come back to the office from different backgrounds and experiences. Some things that were acceptable before the pandemic will not bode well with everyone anymore. This means that HR will take a more active oversight role to address issues as, and when, they arise instead of standing by and letting things take a natural course.

Practical Leadership

Ethical leadership is one of the HR skills that will be in demand in the corporate environment. As much as many companies are looking at return-to-work models, it's not going to be an easy shift. Since people struggled with different challenges during the resulting lockdowns, it's possible that not everyone will be comfortable returning to work right away. Not everyone will be comfortable getting into an elevator with other people as they used to before the pandemic. These are valid concerns that must be considered and addressed by HR. This also means that if the option to choose is available, a lot of employees will prefer to keep working from home.

Thanks to the pandemic, HR must also review leadership behaviors ahead of implementing any return-to-work formula. The reviews are necessary in light of the volatile business environment and also to safeguard the interests of employees. As the workplace evolution aligns with the changing demands of the pandemic, there are many practical challenges that HR must address to prepare their teams for the new business environment.

Effective leadership will revolve around creating supporting systems for HR to manage teams remotely and establishing frameworks for trustworthy remote working models. The first step to succeeding with such a plan is self-assessment. Which essential leadership skills are required? Even though the solutions might vary across industries, some universal leadership skills will always be welcome across the divide.

Below are some important leadership skills that will enable employers to create a safe and accommodating workplace environment post-pandemic:

1. Building Leadership Networks

The leadership role will be important in all aspects of returning to work or the hybrid office. Commit resources to creating, nurturing, and managing leadership relations in different capacities. Whether your team is working from home or not, they should be able to collaborate and support one another.

Effective leadership skills will make it easier for you to conduct leadership roles within the post-pandemic business environment. To this end, you must still rely on tested approaches to ensure that you can match people with the right processes.

2. Empathy in Leadership

There has never been a time in the corporate world when the need for empathy was greater than it is today. Having been pushed into survival mode by the pandemic, it is understandable that most people will be apprehensive of normal interactions when they get back to the working environment. This is where empathetic leadership will come in handy.

New challenges, new concerns, and demands from the workforce can exert a toll on your employees. Your role is to help them manage these emerging issues. Before the pandemic, many people were struggling to establish a healthy work-life balance. Now that they have had a taste of working from home, the lines are even blurrier than before. Throw in the additional challenge of dealing with family members and you have a recipe for chaos.

While the prospect of working from home and the related freedoms are exciting for many employees, there are unintended challenges that you have to find a way to address. Many have struggled with urgent tasks, time, and workload management. In fact, many people end up working longer hours at home than they would in the office. As a leader, you need to stay ahead of such challenges, understand how they affect performance and the overall health of your team, then come up with relatable solutions. Otherwise, your team might become too fatigued to meet their deliverables.

3. Feedback and People Management

The final ingredient is to create a people management system around feedback loops. Whether people are returning to work or working from home, you must prepare for a hybrid business environment that can accommodate the needs of employees in either category, while at the same time supporting the core demands of your organization.

Feedback loops can help you create an open communication platform where teams can share experiences, motivate one another, and, eventually, support team morale. Real-time feedback will go a long way in helping you understand the complex challenges that your team is going through, brainstorm reasonable solutions, and implement them.

This aspect of people management is largely a collaborative approach, with shared input from strategy teams and the employees. If done properly, you will spend less time dealing with orientation concerns, as your team can easily adopt changes because they were mostly their suggestions.

The points discussed above culminate into talent management. Coupled with all the data you have at your disposal from different reporting apps and programs, you should be able to offer the assurances employees need to keep delivering on their goals and remain valuable assets to the organization. All the talk about people management will be futile if you cannot establish real connections with your teams.

At this juncture, we are talking about employee experiences. Using the same approach that design and strategy teams implement to come up with definitive products and services for customers, you can also come up with real solutions for employees. More often, customer-centric teams work backward, starting from the solution and then identifying steps. In the same manner, you can also start from the end. What do your employees need to enhance their engagement and experiences? Once you figure that out, you can work backward from their pain points and identify relevant steps to success.

Creating a Healthy Working Environment

While it's almost impossible to tell when things will go back to normal, or if they ever will, one thing that we are certain about is that at some point people will come to the office. The thought is scary for a lot of people, jarring, and might result in a lot of awkward moments. One of your roles as an ethical leader is to make the transition as smooth as possible for your teams.

Like mental health, failure to prepare appropriate policies to guide the return-to-work formula might bring unpleasant financial and physical challenges. Productivity is great, but a healthy and safe workforce is even better. Let's discuss some changes you can work around below.

1. **A Safe Environment**

Employee safety and health should be at the top of your list of priorities when they return to work. Creating a safe environment is as simple as sticking to the basics. For example, hire professionals for deep-cleaning services to eliminate germs and bacteria. Ensure workspaces are regularly disinfected, clean the air ducts, and get the office carpets shampooed. It doesn't matter that no one might have been using the office for a while, deep cleaning gives everyone peace of mind.

Common areas should be cleaned or disinfected regularly throughout the day. This is one cost center whose budget will be significantly higher in your accounts than before, but it is all for a good cause.

2. Champion Good Hygiene

All the efforts in keeping the workspace clean and convenient for everyone might be futile if it is not replicated at an individual level. You will achieve great success with this initiative with higher employee buy-in. As long as everyone is committed to the plan and follows it through, you should be good to go.

To achieve this, get managers, supervisors, and other team leaders to support this cause and lead by example. Remind them of things that might seem mundane but will play a huge role in keeping the work environment safe, for example, sneezing into their elbow or tissue, regularly washing hands, and other general good hygiene habits. To drive the message home, have posters placed at strategic points in common areas; highlight proper hygiene measures, and remind your staff that it's their collective duty to keep the place safe.

Ensure you have all the necessary hygienic supplies available, including hand sanitizers, soaps, tissues, face masks, paper towels, and disinfectant spray or wipes.

3. Discuss Working Arrangements

If, for strategic reasons or otherwise, you need your team to resume working from the office, you should first ensure there are no alternatives and, where possible, only allow this if it's essential. Hybrid working environments are highly recommended these days, so try to exhaust your options first.

It will be good for morale if employees feel they are involved in decisions that determine how they work during and after the pandemic.

Give them the options and, from there, take the necessary steps to ensure they are comfortable.

Comforts should not be limited to the office. Even if they work from home, check-in with them regularly to ensure they are alright. For remote working, provide any equipment they might need, software, and anything else that can make their working environment at home conducive. Discuss working hours and, more importantly, check on their mental and physical well-being.

4. Recharging Your Team

The fact that people have been working remotely for more than a year means that everyone has probably slid into a personal routine that makes sense to them. Contrary to the normal office routines, a home office might be largely flexible, which means that there might be a struggle when your team returns to work fully. Most importantly, returning to work means that they'll be giving up their flexibility and freedom.

To a large extent, it's only normal to anticipate widespread reluctance to give up remote working. To get around this, you need a phased return-to-work formula. In the early weeks, encourage the team to be flexible with their work hours. The point here is to help them become comfortable working away from their homes first before you make adjustments to their schedules.

Once they are relatively comfortable working from the office, the next step is to get them into a routine. Remember that everyone probably has a personal routine at this point, so getting them back to a standardized routine might not be easy. Some productivity resources might come in handy at this point.

The whole point of returning to work is to ensure that your team gets back to work with the least friction possible. If possible, extend their remote working models further. If they have to come back to the office, schedule some remote working days in their contract so they don't have to be in the office every day.

5. Social Interaction

We spend so much time away from one another, social interaction might not be the easiest thing, yet it is necessary for a normal working environment. Granted, you can't preempt how things will turn out here. Depending on personalities, some employees will be so excited to see their colleagues after a long while they will risk everything to catch up and try to feel normal again. You'll also have those who choose extreme caution, even bordering on social awkwardness.

Whichever the case, you must be the equalizer. Each of these groups has valid concerns that you must address to ensure they feel comfortable working from the office. As you can imagine, those who exercise extreme caution will not be amused when they see others cavorting like it's 2019.

To make your work easier, don't bring everyone back at the same time. You can go by department or even schedule a program such that every department comes to the office once a week without crowding the space.

Think of creative ways to keep people interacting with one another once they get back to the office. Open communication works best and encourages people to speak up and share ideas. You can also create groups around special interests. For example, fitness enthusiasts, foodies, fashionistas, and so on, can create channels on Slack or Telegram, just like sports fans do. These shared activities can help you bring back the rapport and smooth the transition back to the office, especially for those who feel awkward about the whole experience.

One thing you should keep at the back of your mind in these interactions is the need for flexibility. As much as there are many things you can do to help your team reconnect, you should not impose. For social interactions, it's always best if the initiative comes from the active participants, while you can only assume an oversight role or recommendation where necessary.

Finally, this is also a good time to review your procedures and policies. Since the pandemic, pretty much everything about the normal workplace changed. This means that some of your company's best practices might not really cut it in light of the new normal. Why is this important? Well, your team was accustomed to those procedures, they were almost second nature to them. If people come back to work and the same procedures still apply, you might have regular conflicts. The same applies if you change them but your teams have not bought into them.

The top of this list should be how to handle information about COVID-19. What's the procedure? Does someone get days off? How many days do they get? What about those who came into contact with them? What's the procedure for an employee who has taken, or is taking care of an infected person at home?

The virus is still challenging on many fronts, so if you have a confirmed case, you might want to consider allowing extended remote working for the affected individuals. This allows them to recuperate fully without putting everyone else at risk.

Remember that the policies above will only be effective when properly communicated with your teams. Let them know what you are working on, why they are important when they return to work, and how they can implement them. The good news is that these are things that they can even practice at home, so when they return to the office, the transition will be easier.

Chapter 5

High Demand for Antifragile Personalities

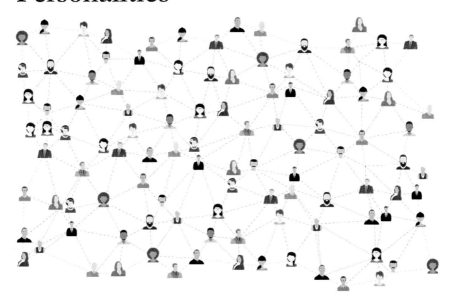

During recruitment, one of the things HR looks at is the candidate's personality. The pandemic affected people differently, and as a result, personality has become one of the most important factors that recruiters look at before hiring. One thing we learned from the pandemic is that the nature of the modern business environment is so dynamic, and for that matter, a culture fit in many organizations would be an employee who is a quick learner.

Quick learning builds resilience in the company making it easier to shift perspectives and align to industry demands when they happen. This doesn't mean that employers are looking for emotionless robots whose decision process revolves around binary choices. It's about being able to bounce back stronger. The business environment during the pandemic was a nightmare for many people with fragile personalities.

Even though companies did the most they could to offer assurances from time to time, people with fragile personalities still struggled.

When recruiting for leadership positions, employer bias will favor individuals with anti-fragile personalities simply because of their resilience and ability to stay positive through periods of uncertainty. It's not just about your ability to stay the course during such times but also how you can influence and offer support to junior employees who might not have the same perspective.

Antifragility is about withstanding the pressure of adversity. The pandemic came with its fair share of uncertain moments, most of which resulted in a lot of ambiguity in decision making. For a business, it's not easy to predict the future when you cannot access your customers because of a lockdown. It gets worse when there's no indication of when the lockdown will be lifted or whether there will be another one. We must also look at the fact that consumer behavior also changed and, even without the lockdowns, people's purchase priorities had shifted to the items they needed for survival.

Antifragility is in demand because employers seek individuals who can help them come out of a crisis unscathed. What's even more interesting about antifragile personalities is that they thrive best during moments of chaos and might even need the chaos. Exposure to stress factors, volatile business environments, randomness, and uncertainty brings out this leadership quality. It is not just about resilience, it is about getting better at responding to chaos over time.

We must be careful not to confuse antifragility with resilience, even though some people use the two terms interchangeably. Antifragility is about coming out of the chaos better than before. It means performing at a higher level than before. Resilience, on the other hand, is about withstanding the pressure of adversity.

Nothing in life is permanent. Therefore, in the business environment, adversity creates an opportunity to ride the ups and downs. It is proof that, like everything else in life, the business environment exists in a wave. There will be moments of growth, moments of chaos, and, at times, lull moments where nothing particularly exciting happens.

But, why does the antifragile personality crave chaos? Why does it only shine during tumultuous moments? Well, one of the innate abilities that we have is our ability to learn and do better. This might be a good time to cue Kelly Clarkson's famous lyric, "what doesn't kill you makes you stronger." Exposure to difficult moments can make you stronger and build your character.

The antifragile personality is great for leadership because you can also inspire your team to change their perspectives and start seeing things the way you do. When people trust in their leader, they can become resilient over time. This is because leaders instill that sense of assurance that the difficult moments won't last forever. They encourage you to persevere and be prepared to hit the ground running as soon as the dust settles. They offer psychological security and create a safe environment within which their teams can embrace adversity.

Psychological security is of the utmost importance because, even though exposure to adversity can push employees out of their comfort zones, it would be irresponsible to expose everyone to adversity and difficult moments, hoping that they will be okay. As a leader, you must understand that your team might not be as strong-willed as you are. Some of your employees might have personalities so fragile they experience a complete meltdown at the first whiff of adversity and shut down altogether. For this reason, you must learn how to address difficult conversations, how to talk to people about them, and offer assurances.

Leadership the Antifragile Way

Antifragile isn't just about staying positive through difficult experiences. Blind optimism can have far worse outcomes than facing reality. It is about openly admitting that things are not working. Once you evaluate all possible scenarios and realize that they can't be salvaged, you inform your team, highlight the lessons you can learn from that situation, and use the pain as a platform to grow and become better. Antifragile is also about embracing failure as a normal part of any experience.

What's more interesting about antifragility is the fact that it correlates with fragility. For example, during the pandemic, the fragile approach to life means isolation and following the laid down safety protocols as advised by different experts. Apart from that, you must also rationalize your concerns, especially where sustainability is involved, whether it's your business, customers, family, or team members.

The pandemic stretched everyone to unimaginable depths, and in many organizations, some business processes thrived despite the unfortunate experiences unfolding worldwide. As an antifragile leader, below are some useful strategies you can follow to help your team get through difficult moments:

1. **Dialogue**

Earlier on we discussed the importance of employee engagement and how it helps to keep them focused and productive even amidst the chaos of the pandemic and the fact that they are all working remotely. Have an open conversation with them. Explain the situation and, more importantly, the magnitude of it.

One of the reasons why the gap between leaders and their teams becomes a problem in many organizations is because leaders don't create a platform where employees can see the reality as they see it. Unfortunately, when things are not working, there's only so much that you can do to shield people from the truth.

Open and honest conversations help you eliminate biases and make you believable to your employees. Remember that every household felt the pinch of the pandemic differently, so without talking to your employees, it's impossible for them to reconcile the company's reality and the reality of their personal lives. Dialogue makes it easier to connect with their pain and their strengths, and together, you can forge a perspective of the future that gives them hope regardless of the unfolding chaos. This is also a good time to deconstruct some of the myths and rumors going on about the pandemic or the future of the company.

2. Future Plans

The conversations above help you come to terms with your new reality. From there, the next step is to plan for the future. It is about moving from where you are to the next phase, and preparing and redefining what must be done to get there. It's about replacing unhealthy behaviors with new ones that will help you do and become better.

Review your present predicament and discuss some of the challenges your teams are currently facing. You might also have to rethink your business processes. For example, what is it about your current situation that you wouldn't wish to experience in the near future? What do you crave right now that would improve your situation?

As you plan for the future, you must realize that everyone else is going through a different struggle that you might not know about. These differences can pull people apart, even though they are working together. As a leader, you must find a way to bring everyone together. Help them connect to your vision. Help them understand why it's important to the organization and how it will benefit them. Shared goals are an easy way to get people to buy into an idea.

Working through the pandemic, collective responsibility will make it easier to discuss and implement changes. This is what you get from shared goals. Collaboration also offers psychological security and safety, which is great for the overall well-being of your team. The best way to achieve this is to welcome different perspectives and help people realize that they are part of the solution and their contribution is valued.

The final step in antifragile leadership is to be conscious and mindful of the dynamics of yours and the lives of your employees. A resilient workforce is one that will resist and withstand the pressures of the pandemic chaos but will largely remain unchanged. This means that when faced with a similar problem in the future, you'll still face the same challenges. An antifragile workforce, on the other hand, does more than withstand the chaos, it gets better, better equipped at dealing with that problem in the future. An antifragile workforce might only be shocked or frustrated by a problem worse than the one they overcame.

Prioritize Diversity and Inclusion Initiatives

Social justice in the corporate environment has been a contentious subject for many years. Corporations have often chosen to remain silent when the conversation heats up on inclusion or diversity for fear of backlash and outrage from the public in case they misread the mood. However, they can't afford to sit on the fence anymore. Social media has empowered the public and given them an active voice on such matters. From time to time companies are called out on discriminating policies, forcing their leadership into crisis meetings to find amicable solutions.

As the pressures of the pandemic became widespread, the push for diversity and inclusive initiatives increased worldwide. Employers must now find ways of improving their existing policies or, where none existed, create clearly defined policies on diversity and inclusion. Contrary to what had been largely existent before, the work doesn't stop at policy. Employers must walk the talk or face the wrath of a woke society.

Employers must also make sure that remote working does not create diversity or inclusion problems. For example, there's the concern among some employees that working from home might mean they miss out on some important meetings or get overlooked for opportunities in favor of those who show up at the office frequently. While this might be a simple example, some employers might actually marginalize a section of their employees using flimsy excuses like these ones.

The whole point of inclusion is to ensure that all employees enjoy the same rights and benefits whether they are working from the office or at home. You must also go the extra mile and address such concerns when they arise, because even though they might seem unreasonable, ignoring them creates an information vacuum. If an employee is overlooked for an opportunity and feels it was awarded to someone who, in their opinion, didn't deserve it, the unreasonable reason might create more problems for the company. In the court of public opinion, once the employee shares their experience on social media, there's not much that the company can do to change the narrative.

Once something is shared online, people often get sentimental and in such moments logic is the last thing most people think about. The company's image will be tarnished, and by the time the spectacle is over, the damage could be irreparable. This is why you must stay ahead of such situations and address them with the urgency they deserve. As long as people are working remotely, you have limited control over some of their decisions.

It's easy for remote workers to feel that they are unheard, ignored, or isolated from company resources, whether this is true or not. Naturally, an employee might feel insecure when they feel left out of decisions that affect them. It is also normal, when you consider the psychological impact the pandemic has had on employees at a personal level, for some people to feel marginalized, even though it might not be the case. That feeling might be the culmination of personal struggles and challenges that are unrelated to the company yet could spark an outburst that ends up costing your company in the long run.

To address such issues and avoid unnecessary confrontations, you should learn how to preempt problematic scenarios. People have different personalities and their responses to social isolation can be extreme from time to time. The impact of social isolation in the pandemic has been highlighted in many HR forums as one of the challenges employers must address going forward. You should learn how to identify situations where employees feel they are marginalized, especially around common situations like ageism, sexism, and racism. Learn how to identify conscious and unconscious aspects of bias; recognize them and do all you can to eliminate bias. Don't just learn, encourage other managers to learn and impart the same knowledge to their teams.

Once you learn some of the factors that make your employees feel marginalized, talk to them about it, and remind them of your commitment to making the workplace better. Support individual employees as much as you support supervisors and provide all the resources they need to be productive. Where possible, reach out to individuals and find out whether they are getting all the support they need to work from home. Find out their concerns and listen to their suggestions on how to solve the problems.

In a diverse workforce, some inappropriate behavior might creep in from time to time. This is normal in every organization. Even though what might be considered inappropriate might be explicit or implied, you should clamp down on such behaviors as soon as you identify them. Ignoring them sends the message that it's either allowed or someone can get away with it.

Going forward, it's in your best interest to learn how to correct behaviors properly. While people might say or do some inappropriate things from time to time, you might not know their motivations. As much as you might reprimand or even punish them, it's good to try and find out why they did it, in case the underlying problem is bigger than you had earlier thought. If someone does something wrong the first time, you might take it lightly and assume it was an unconscious mistake. However, if the same happens a second time, that's a pattern that should not be tolerated. Address the matter in public so that people know it's wrong, but do not call the individual out. Instead, hold a private session and discuss it with them and, where possible, offer the necessary coaching or support.

Encourage your employees to reach out privately and talk about their concerns whenever they feel marginalized. Remote working can make you feel isolated and build up anxiety. It's important during these difficult times that you pay more attention to your employees at the individual level. That's the only way to stay ahead of such problems.

Chapter 6:

Nudging Over Policing

How do you get your team to support and implement initiatives? The best support comes when people understand what is expected of them and why it's in their best interest to follow through on the outlined steps. This is an aspect of behavioral economics known as nudge theory that has been widely used to champion behavioral change in individuals and groups.

Nudging has always proven more productive than policing employees, hence its importance in managing work during and after the pandemic. Many people have worked away from the offices for more than a year. During this time, it's fair to expect that they developed certain behavioral changes. So if they were to return to work today, their responses would not be the same as they were in 2019 before the pandemic.

The beauty of nudge theory is that you can use it to explain, understand, or even study behavioral influences and change patterns, especially to distinguish healthy from unhealthy behavior. Ideally, you should reward or encourage healthy behavior, while at the same time try to correct unhealthy ones. Behavioral nudges don't have to be extreme. In most cases, they are simple things that we take for granted, but the more we interact with them, they become a part of our subconscious, altering behavior patterns.

Individual capabilities, knowledge, features, and attitudes make it easier to adopt behavioral nudges because they gradually grow on you. On the other hand, the same features would probably make you ignore autocratic policing approaches. The concept of nudging is to gradually help you understand your environment, and as its reality settles, you appreciate it for what it is. This is why nudging works over policing. Policing ignores your reality and is simply a set of instructions that must be followed or you face the consequences.

Pretty much, we can say that nudging contextualizes your experience. By giving them choices, you encourage employees to make decisions that would be most ideal, not just for them, in the context of their environment, for the greater good of everyone.

Post-pandemic change management will be one of the biggest challenges employers have to deal with. Assuming that people resume work fully, or in whichever capacity, many employees will need coaching on several aspects of personal development. In this regard, your ethical leadership skills will help you keep them motivated.

Nudging is actually an effective way to improve decision making in the workplace. In times of stress, or when people are exhausted, logical decision making tends to break down. This is something many employers will experience when people stop working from home. Instead of forcing them to make rational decisions, nudging can influence them to make the right decisions. This process relies on simple, yet effective, changes in the employee's surroundings that don't necessarily carry huge financial commitments or legislative procedure.

A common example that has been used effectively in many places is displaying healthy food within a consumer's line of sight, instead of banning junk food outright. Most people might not realize it, but the fact that they see healthy food regularly could influence them to be more conscious about what they eat, and over time, they will choose that over junk food. If, however, you decided to impose bans on junk food, people would simply go and look for it elsewhere in defiance, which defeats the purpose.

How to Implement Nudges Effectively

Even though nudging is a great tool for modeling behavioral changes in the workplace, you must be pragmatic in your approach. Like other good things, too much of something or using it in the wrong way can lead to unfortunate experiences. While nudging can encourage positive behavior among your employees, it can also be quite efficient in modeling unhealthy behavior. Here are some simple guidelines to ensure you use nudges to model the right behaviors:

1. **Transparency**

Try to model nudges in a manner that isn't misleading, imposing, or overwhelming to your employees. As much as you are trying to encourage them to adopt some behaviors, the process should be transparent. For example, it's possible that not every employee will get on board. In this case, and since you are not imposing behavior change on them, make it easier for such employees to opt out of the process.

The whole point of this process is to encourage employees to realize the benefit of behavioral change. If you have to force them to see it, then clearly, something's not right, and it's best if you allow those who were uncomfortable to walk away.

For example, one of the areas where nudges are often misused is promotional offers where people are required to read the fine print. Naturally, most people don't read the fine print and only realize too late when they already missed out on the offer or have to incur some expense to claim their offer. At this point, whatever choice the individual makes, they are already at a disadvantage.

Many companies come up with procedures and make the exit process quite cumbersome, it eventually feels like it was meant to benefit them, instead of the intended users. In the workplace, nudging can only be effective if, apart from encouraging employees to act a certain way, they also espouse the company's goals and culture.

2. Appeal to Social Interests

Another way to make nudges effective is to model them around social interests. People naturally crave a sense of belonging. This explains why you find different interest groups at work. The sports fanatics tend to hang out together, the yoga enthusiasts, tech groups, and so on. Such interactions are built on relationships.

To this end, consider creating nudges that appeal to these interest groups. When someone in a group is doing something new, everyone around them might be interested and will want to find out why they are doing it and the benefits. They will discuss it, and you can be certain that more people will buy into the idea, simply so that they don't feel left out. Interest groups are generally bound by some unwritten rules, and none of the members would want to break them and feel like the odd one out. You can use these social interests to bring people together by encouraging subtle behavioral changes between them.

3. Model Agreeability

Agreeability builds on the gains of social interests. Employers have used this tactic for years to get results. Once you have an influential person on board, use this reassurance to encourage everyone else to follow suit. This is pretty much the concept of influencer marketing as widely used on social media.

People draw some reassurance in knowing that if someone they look up to, or one of their peers, is doing something then they probably should do the same thing too. This is usually a good option in a situation where people harbor some doubts or uncertainty about processes or procedures.

It might also work for you from an organizational point of view. For example, when the lockdowns were initiated, many companies were unsure whether they could manage to keep operations going with everyone working from home. This was uncharted territory for a lot of companies who had never considered remote working. However, slowly, they started learning from what other companies were doing and modeled the same structures for their employees. Before long, working from home was working for everyone.

Before modeling agreeability, however, you need to ensure you have valid data that the approach has been successful when adopted elsewhere. You also need to know how it was implemented, what challenges were experienced, and how they were addressed.

4. Likability

In group dynamics, people generally have a burning desire to be liked. For this reason, they will easily change their behavior if it means that they get to earn favor with everyone else. The desire to be liked can also encourage employees to change their behavior so that they can belong to a certain group or clique that already behaves that way.

This is almost similar to the concept of agreeability, just that in this case, you take a keen interest in the individual's desire for likability. To model this effectively, you need to understand the shared goals between the target employees and the individuals they are taking after. Other than goals, it's also easier to nudge individuals with shared beliefs or who perhaps share a religion.

Within these substructures, try to encourage individuals to understand the benefits of membership, and at the same time, highlight the disadvantages of errant or deviant behavior within their ranks.

As you follow the procedures outlined above, you must also embrace the learning curve that ensues. The thing about championing behavior change is that there's so much to learn in the process because people are different and won't always respond or react in the same manner. Where your approaches are welcome, consistency and commitment to the cause will help you realize further uptake.

Ultimately, even though nudges can help you model behavior change, you must be careful not to misuse them. If the nudge strategies work for you, there's the potential risk of using this approach to solve most, if not all challenges you encounter in the office. That being said, you should be careful on how to monitor and implement nudges. If you rely on them too much, people become used to the pattern and after a while they can become ineffective.

Enhance Employee Experiences

When it comes to improving employee experiences with nudges, it's usually the simple things that matter. This pretty much works for most human interactions. Let's take the example of the seatbelt in your car. You learned its importance in driving school and every other place where road safety is discussed. However, for some reason, a lot of people still forget to put on their seatbelts. To handle this problem, car manufacturers created that annoying sound that reminds you to buckle up. So, you can either listen to that sound throughout your journey or simply belt up and enjoy a peaceful ride. Subconsciously, you'll reach for the belt.

These simple changes go a long way in encouraging good behavior, and that's how it should be done even at work. To implement successful nudges, you must first identify clear targets for change. Now that people are returning to work, one of your targets will be to ensure the workplace remains a healthy and safe environment for all employees. This means that you might have picked up on some behaviors during video interactions with your employees while they were working from home which might be problematic when they come to work.

You are also aware that not everyone will adhere to social distancing and other guidelines to prevent the spread of the virus when they resume work from the office. This is true because of different aspects of social dynamics. These are the kind of problems for which healthy behavior change can be modeled.

For this process to be effective in enhancing employee experiences, you need to understand their daily routines and experiences. This gives you a better context of their decision-making process. While some behaviors might appear unhealthy, it makes sense to follow up with the employee and find out why they make sense to them. Learning their pain points makes it easier for you to address their needs.

Finally, before implementing nudges, you must find out and eliminate barriers to the desired changes. Barriers could be social, physical, or even psychological. From the unique challenges that people experienced during the pandemic, one thing you can be certain about is that many people will have psychological barriers to behavior change. The fear, uncertainty, and, in some cases, trauma from the tragic loss of loved ones might not be easy to overcome.

You will have to use all the tools at your disposal to make things work. One of the emerging trends in HR post-pandemic will be the use of data analytics. This goes hand in hand with the remote working models that have been in use for more than a year. You have since gathered a lot of data on employee experiences which you can use to improve their experiences.

Ideally, nudges should be personalized and precise, especially in a work environment that is embracing the hybrid office model. They are more effective when presented as personal reminders to do something that benefits their well-being in the long run. For example, a simple reminder to take a break from work can make a big difference.

When people return to work, instead of having the water dispenser at a central point, you can replace it with small water bottles on their desks. While someone might feel too lazy to walk to the dispenser, they can easily grab that bottle on their desk. Another benefit to this is that as they drink from the bottle, they'll need to use the bathroom frequently which keeps them walking, breaking the monotony of sitting down throughout the day.

Work with your tech teams to build subtle nudges into productivity tools like the Microsoft Office suite you use. Encourage them to set "out of office" reminders so that they are not bogged down with work once they are out of the office.

Further on the hybrid office setup, your tech team can also go a step further and create brief video previews of new features before rolling out an update. This should pop up as a notification allowing employees to prepare psychologically for the changes to be implemented. Many people usually struggle with updates that push wholesale changes to their systems.

Behavior change isn't necessarily about using the data and knowledge at your disposal but implementing subtle interventions that appeal to basic human needs and behaviors. On the employee's side, these implementations help them realize that the company takes a keen interest in their well-being. For management, you get actionable information on engagement and how to improve performance over time.

Nudges are a proactive approach that, when implemented effectively, will not just improve employee experiences but also their resilience and your employee retention targets. Communicate your expectations clearly, and encourage employees to reach out if they need further clarification or if they have any concerns, especially on personal data and privacy.

Chapter 7

Skill Mapping: Looking for Adjacent Skills

HR has evolved so much since the pandemic in a bid to meet the present challenges. For this reason, we've seen a major shift from job-based to skill-based HR. This is important in that it helps employers understand the skill composition in the job market, in order to prepare for the future of work. Coming out of the pandemic, one thing that's evident is that there might be a shortage of some special skills, especially where experience is highly sought after.

Today, employers are more interested in wholesome leadership skills. This means someone who cannot just manage a team but can also balance short and long-term goals, inspire, encourage, and offer the necessary operational and strategic support at different levels. Even though it's almost impossible to predict how the business environment will be affected by the pandemic, one thing that we can aptly predict is a transformative working experience.

As the business environment evolves, the need to master new skills and create new roles to handle the changes becomes more apparent by the day. In retrospect, a lot of people have also had to rethink their careers and the roles they play in their organizations. People seek opportunities in organizations that can make them feel appreciated. Therefore, even the composition of the job market is changing and, as many people are looking for employment opportunities, their requirements will not be the same as they were in 2019.

Employers must now take responsibility and usher employees into the new business environment by offering them support and resources for professional growth. This is possible through skill mapping. One of the objectives of skill mapping is to provide professional training that prepares employees for the dynamic shift in the business environment by imparting skills and competencies that help them meet the business needs.

Understanding Skill Mapping

The concept of skill mapping is to give you a glimpse of all the skills present in the business at a particular time. For every position or job description in the organization, you should have a clear depiction of the soft and hard skills available in the organization. You should also know what skills are missing, and at what levels, so that you can either train some employees to fill the gaps or hire new employees.

Skill mapping is best addressed by referencing jobs over positions. This is important because positions are flexible and, depending on the underlying tasks, they can change from time to time. A job, on the other hand, is an industry standard that is widely recognized everywhere.

Since the pandemic, companies have had to change from people management to skill management. Instead of looking to hire people, you should focus on filling skill gaps in the organization. Skill management is actually one of the emerging trends that will help in reshaping the course of HR after the pandemic. There are many technological tools available that HR can use to preempt skill gaps not just in the organization but also across the industry.

Once you anticipate skill shortages in the future, you can take steps to train employees or encourage them to adapt to their jobs faster. The bonus for the company is that by encouraging people within the organization to rise to the occasion you save on hiring costs, which, depending on the success or failure of your hiring process, can be too costly especially when you factor in the challenge of cultural fit.

In a rapidly evolving job market, it's always good to stay informed on market trends and anticipate how skill availability will respond to external forces like the pandemic. Skill mapping gives you deeper insight into the personal skills and competencies of every employee within your organization, including their weaknesses, knowledge gaps, and strengths that you can tap into. This can also become an informative tool for internal growth and development discussions with your team and useful for helping them become aware of their strengths and weaknesses.

Importance to Organizational Planning

Skill mapping to HR is what financial statements like balance sheets are to the organization. Financial statements present information on the financial health of the organization. Similarly, skill mapping helps HR understand an organization's position in terms of valuable human capital. Apart from highlighting your skill gaps, it can also act as a valuable evaluation tool that might come in handy when reviewing benefits and remuneration packages.

From the information obtained, you can easily identify redundancies and work around them. An example from your analysis will be whether each job currently present in the organization is necessary for driving the company forward. This will also inform your needs in the event that a recruitment exercise is necessary. Since you already know the experiences and skills lacking in your organization, you can refine your desired candidate profiles to finite details.

This exercise will also be useful not just for planning training exercises but to ensure they are effective. For example, you don't have to bundle all employees in a training exercise. This becomes a waste because some of them already possess the skills and will feel their time would be best used elsewhere. Training sessions should be organized according to the demands of the job description and the skill profile of the employees presently undertaking that job.

Another area where skill mapping will be useful is in a needs assessment. There are instances where employees might suggest or even formally request some training exercises. While this is commendable and encouraged, you must decide whether they really need that training. Training programs should be built around relevance so that you don't waste resources training employees for skills that might never be relevant to your organization.

Both business and personal skills are necessary in every organization at the moment. With skill mapping, you get better insight into individual employees' potential in terms of internal job mobility. This is a cost-effective approach to bridging skill gaps within the organization. Naturally, you might also benefit from bridging the gap between professions. For example, you might need a financial perspective in the HR department. Instead of hiring someone in that capacity, you can promote one of the junior employees within the financial department who has delivered exemplary performance over the years and has proven their leadership skills.

This method of developing employee skills, either from training or experience, makes it easier for you to identify ideal candidates within the organization each time you need to fill an open position. This is also good for morale because employees are aware of the potential for growth in the organization. It's usually demoralizing when companies seek external candidates to fill positions when the existing employees can do the job.

Ideally, skill mapping brings objectivity into decision making in the organization. All your decisions around promotion, training, compensation, and other tasks within your oversight role are informed by measurable and precise data. This also makes it easier to communicate your expectations to employees, so they understand how they fit in with the company's plan for future growth.

Future Outlook in Skill Trends

As we anticipate people returning to work, HR must also prepare for emerging trends in skill management. At the moment, almost every company, including those that never planned for or needed remote working models, has some plan in place. While we can be optimistic about people fully returning to work, we cannot tell with 100% certainty whether this will happen. Therefore, there will be a demand for new skills to match the needs of a remote working economy.

The pandemic was an eye-opener in that most jobs don't really require physical interaction. Advancements in technology and digitization of work systems made this realization more apparent by adding credibility to the push towards reducing, if not eliminating, unnecessary physical interactions.

Besides, since people started working from home many employees have reported better experiences with their work. For some, working from home allows them to spend more time with their families, something that had become a major stress point in the corporate environment over the years. Citing lack of time, many people often made the decision to either give up on the family way altogether and focus on their careers or take a sabbatical from work. With remote working, employees can now enjoy the best of both worlds and, buoyed by different support systems, the outlook for employment can be wholesome once again.

Remote working has also mandated the need to reinvent some business processes. Take the healthcare system, for example. In the first few weeks of the pandemic, rapid changes were implemented that would probably still be a long shot today. In-person consultations with doctors have been replaced by video link consultations. Before the pandemic, rolling out such changes to the masses was often met with criticism and challenges from time to time. However, when pushed to the wall, we made it happen.

Even though such changes have been effective in protecting the lives of frontline healthcare workers, it also means that they must learn how to accurately diagnose patients remotely. Now, that's a skill gap that HR in the medical sector will actively look into.

The reality is that many businesses will have to retrain their employees to equip them with new skills for the remote economy. An important skill that employers must pay attention to is empathy. Without physical interaction, it might be difficult for employees to read the customer's mood and empathize accordingly.

You must also prepare for drastic supply chain changes and the impact that they might have on your workforce. Over the years, many industries have moved production and sourcing channels closer to the end users thereby helping them streamline the supply chain and realize more cost savings. This trend will persist in the future with many companies considering regionalization or localization of production and sourcing. Apart from making their business more efficient, bringing the business closer to end users also makes it cheaper for their customers.

This push to restructure the supply chain also means that some industries that were massively outsourced overseas could see more business moving back inland. The point here is to create more value along domestic supply chains, especially in vital industries like pharmaceuticals, food, and agriculture.

Analyze your projections for the future to determine how such changes might affect the composition of your workforce and how to realign and prepare for the future. You might have to grow your workforce to match the speed of change in your supply chain, which is a critical reskilling exercise that might be influenced by external factors beyond your control.

How to Prepare for the Future

Companies have to restructure the workforce to have a better chance of surviving the dynamic changes. Let's discuss some approaches you can use to achieve this below:

First, you have to understand the new skills your business will need in the future. From skill mapping, you should know where your company is lagging behind and the skills you'll need to push the company forward in the future. Assess different roles and their relevance to the growth potential of your business.

Which behavioral changes will be required for your growth and success in the future? How many people will you need in each capacity? Now that most businesses have understood the rigors of remote working, will you need everyone to return to work fully? How do these decisions affect employment contracts?

With the information above, assess the skills needed for your growth model and engage your team on the need to upskill in a manner that benefits both their interests and the company's needs. Some jobs will evolve so much that they might be completely redefined. Discuss this with employees beforehand to prepare them psychologically, and make the transition smoother.

Social and emotional skills, cognitive skills, adaptability, resilience, and digital skills will be highly sought after in the future. Most of these skills were often complementary skills in the workplace before the pandemic. However, they will be in high demand in future workplaces as more people work remotely. These are areas where you should consider training for your employees right away. Another critical skill is change management. Even though the possible worst-case scenarios of the COVID-19 pandemic are behind us, the rate and magnitude of change experienced in the workplace since 2020 are proof that employers need to invest in change management training for their employees to mitigate any further challenges in the future.

Many companies that have implemented reskilling strategies in the past are usually able to anticipate and fill skill gaps better than those that haven't. The need for reskilling isn't only as a result of the pandemic; it might also be in response to change in business strategies or business models. When a company is acquired or restructuring through a merger, reskilling is often necessary because these procedures eventually involve changes in strategic direction.

Even if your reskilling approach isn't as successful as you had imagined, you are still in a better position than a company that did not attempt it in the first place. One thing you learn from reskilling, whether you succeed or not, is that it helps you rethink your approach to role changes and disruption in the future. If your approach failed, you review the reasons behind the failure and make plans on how to do better next time. This leaves you better placed to manage change than waiting for the future to unfold and react to it.

You should also understand that reskilling is not a process you implement once and forget about it. Even if the pandemic is over and people resume work, you still need to future-proof your business.

Whether you need to redeploy some employees or if you only need talent reskilling, lessons learned in the process will help in capacity building in the future and help you keep the company running in the event of disruptive events.

Finally, one of the best ways to implement reskilling strategies is a small-scale approach. It's practically easier for smaller companies to reskill than large companies with thousands of employees. Granted, large companies have more resources at their disposal compared to smaller companies, reskilling isn't always one of the smoothest experiences.

One possible reason why reskilling is easier in smaller companies is the ease of implementing agile practices. Decision making in large organizations is often slowed down by bureaucratic procedures. The sheer size of small organizations makes leadership simpler and decision making faster. Besides, if you have a smaller team for reskilling, it's easier to address their needs on a case-by-case basis. In large organizations, many approaches revolve around standardization because of the sheer size of the workforce.

That being said, you don't have to struggle simply because yours is a large organization. For successful reskilling, you need to approach this with a different strategy. Analyze the number of employees who need reskilling and determine working clusters. Now while people are still working from home, you can approach this one department at a time to give you a better perspective of progress.

The point of a small-scale approach is to give you more insight not just into the skill deficiencies but also to follow progress keenly and prioritize the changing needs of your employees alongside organizational objectives. Of course, this doesn't mean that having a large organization automatically suggests failure. Many large organizations have reskilled employees before and realized significant success. It all comes down to planning and execution. It might be difficult, but it's not impossible.

Chapter 8

Lean on Technology for Automated HR Processes

For ages, there have always been calls for in-depth technological integration in HR. Some organizations have achieved significant success while others struggled and probably went back to traditional HR. The integration has largely been problematic because HR has predominantly remained an in-person department in many organizations, at least until the pandemic happened.

Since then, many organizations were forced to fast-track the integration to meet the growing demand and urgency of remote working models. Tech support services were largely deployed to support employees in their business activities and to ensure that they still had access to HR support services in different capacities.

While many companies cited insufficient financial resources and support systems for a full implementation before the pandemic, somehow most of them overcame these challenges during the pandemic and adopted different tech systems into HR.

The need for companies to invest in HR technology was necessitated by the desire to improve employee experiences during the pandemic when they had limited or no access to in-person support from HR. Apart from that, with many people working from home, traditional HR systems oversight almost became redundant and relied on telecommunication programs like Zoom, which basically don't offer any relevant information other than communication. Thus, HR needed data-driven solutions to refine the oversight role and ensure there was no vacuum in HR services as the global workforce was nearly crippled by the pandemic.

During the period when people have been working remotely, the use of technology in HR has taken different forms. Even though oversight was the primary objective for most implementations, unique challenges experienced by employees meant that somehow tech support systems had to find a way to make employees a part of the integration. In this regard, HR's concern included connecting with employees, engaging, measuring engagement, and drawing useful inferences from the interactions.

Technology has also played a big role in ensuring that HR can still conduct the traditional roles of recruiting and onboarding new employees, which pretty much eased the unemployment crisis that was imminent and helped many organizations survive the pandemic. In cases where tech support systems were implemented on a trial basis, many employers soon realized the effectiveness and value of these systems and scaled up their technology to allow HR more room to effectively handle their roles.

HR technology helped many businesses manage the initial stress as a result of the entire workforce suddenly working from home. This was possible because of access to analytical data from different programs in application, which also made it easier for companies to keep core services and departments running albeit remotely.

HR technology has so far been useful in people management by helping employers manage staffing decisions in a market where a shortage of skilled labor has been the norm. We can expect more advancements in HR technology beyond the pandemic with more companies investing in transformative and sustainable technology that will become the foundation on which future work models are built. That being said, employers must also make sure that technological advancements in HR are aligned with their organizational growth needs and objectives.

The ease with which technology helped employers manage uncertainty during the pandemic is laudable and one of the reasons why this sector deservedly needs more investment in the future. Going forward, there will be increased demand for systems that collect more information, provide refined analytics, and offer more value in terms of employee metrics. With this information, employers have more actionable data that can be used to make crucial decisions.

Evolution of HR Roles

All business functions were significantly affected by the pandemic, but none more than human resources as companies struggled to remain afloat amidst the chaos. During the period characterized by lockdowns and other containment measures, HR went through a lot of changes, especially in the management processes. Most changes to the work dynamics were attributed to the fact that more people were working remotely.

Apart from guiding and leading the entire workforce through a digital remote working environment, HR also had to learn at the same time how to reinvent their roles and integrate with technology where possible. This means that as much as HR workers are change agents and will champion reskilling and other practices to align business models with the future of the working environment, you must also be prepared to learn and handle tasks that you normally would not have to do. This is how the role of HR during the pandemic evolved.

The internet and technology played a huge role in the evolution of HR roles. Let's have a look at some of the changing roles you must contend with as we navigate uncertain business environment:

1. Technological Advancement

Remote working models are leveraged on the benefits of technological advancement. The pandemic induced an immediate shift to remote working, which created, or increased demand in companies that already had the models in place, the need for airtight, intuitive systems. Ideal systems are built for easy access by employers and employees alike, regardless of their location.

As change agents, HR must learn and understand the new technology before overseeing training and implementation exercises for employees. Before a company adopts a new system, HR must shortlist, select, learn, and test the system. This means that HR will continually assume IT specialist roles from time to time.

To make this easier, you must collaborate with your IT teams to make your learning process seamless and, from there, gain the support skills necessary to help employees through regular challenges. The only issues that should be escalated to the IT department are things that might be beyond your skill set, at least for now.

2. New Recruitment Processes

Some companies had already experimented with virtual recruitment even before the pandemic and had an idea of what to expect. Unfortunately, most companies do not fall in this category and had to hurriedly embrace virtual recruitment to fill the skill gaps in different departments during the chaotic pandemic experience.

The hurried transition comes with unique challenges and concerns because of the inability to experience the candidate's presence. It's not easy to manage an entire recruitment process from planning to selection and hiring. Companies were also forced to conduct onboarding processes online. The entire recruitment experience without an in-person interaction is rather awkward, especially for HR managers who excel at interpersonal interactions.

Naturally, as much as HR teams are learning to cope with the new normal, it's not easy to navigate the challenges of running an entire job fair and hiring exercise online. Somehow, it feels like the virtual experience robs you of the element of authenticity.

That being said, we cannot ignore an idea whose time is nigh. Virtual recruitment is here to stay, and the best you can do in your capacity is to improve the existing systems in an attempt to retain some authenticity to them. Your best chance at succeeding with virtual recruitment is to improve communication and engagement skills, making it easier to interact with new hires and ease their nerves as soon as possible.

Remember that as much as you might struggle with the lack of personality in virtual recruitment, potential hires might be equally frustrated or nervous, so it's up to you to level the playing field and create a comfortable environment for recruitment that allows them to feel at ease and present the best version of themselves.

3. Team Management

Working from home is great, at least for employees. They enjoy the freedom to work flexible hours and within a comfortable environment without dealing with pesky colleagues or feeling under pressure from supervisors who are always lurking over their shoulders. Unfortunately, for HR, managing teams remotely isn't always as pleasant an experience as employees might be having.

To be fair, the conversation around remote work models had been going on before the pandemic, and some forward-thinking companies were already experimenting with different modes of implementation. Unfortunately, even they were caught off guard and suddenly the luxury of time was gone.

Suddenly, HR had to learn on the job how to manage teams remotely. While at the same time they were dealing with various challenges arising from implementation and providing assurances to an agitated and worried workforce about the uncertainties around their jobs. Well, it's been more than a year since remote working started, and a lot of HR teams have gotten used to it. Some have improved their management systems by integrating innovative software solutions to make the process more efficient.

More employers intend to encourage their teams to work remotely even after the pandemic, which means that HR might become a partially or fully remote function in the future. With this in mind, the in-demand skills in the HR market will also evolve with more companies preferring HR managers who possess skills relevant to remote employee management.

Frontline Privacy Guards

The shift to virtual working models created a new concern in the corporate environment: employee and organization privacy. Initially, as soon as lockdowns were initiated, many companies resorted to video apps like Zoom and Skype to engage their teams and keep the workflow going. It wasn't long before reports of hackers infiltrating webinars and executive meetings became widespread, raising concerns over the security and privacy of such interactions.

Apart from that, employers have invested in data analytics solutions alongside various HR technologies to help them understand their teams better. Many employees are concerned that too much of their information is available online and some of the data analytics solutions implemented by their employers are too intrusive.

The challenge for HR, therefore, is how to protect employee and company information online. This isn't easy considering that IT security isn't exactly one of HR's strongest skills. They must work closely with IT teams and, even so, still contend with integration bottlenecks between the two independent departments. For companies that are not big enough to have an independent IT team, the solution might be outsourcing tech support services to experts.

Whichever approach you use, you must understand the applicable regulations on data privacy and the confines of ethical use to which you can put the data obtained from your employees. Clearly, this isn't one of HR's traditional roles, but you must adapt quickly and act accordingly, lest you get sued for irresponsible handling of private employee data in the event of a breach.

HR Technology and Post-Pandemic Challenges

The world over, everyone struggled financially, physically, or mentally through the pandemic. While these challenges were mostly at a personal level, the impact on employee productivity makes them interesting focus points for employers. This explains why HR teams assumed crisis management roles during the ensuing lockdowns. Other than ensuring that the core functions of companies were not tragically affected, HR teams also had to look after the mental health and general well-being of employees from their remote locations. Below are three important challenges that HR teams had to deal with and might continue to address as the pandemic progresses:

1. Policy Changes

The business environment keeps evolving and with it the need to update policies from time to time. So many policies were affected by the pandemic, and it's up to HR, together with legal and risk management teams, to update them and ensure they are communicated with all employees for compliance.

It's not been easy to keep up with the policy changes, especially since most changes come down to intra-organizational interpretation instead of industry standards. The other challenge is that HR practically doesn't have sufficient time to make all the policy changes as many companies are already working on return-to-work programs. This means that some policy changes will be communicated to employees on the go making the process of reintegration into the office from remote working a delicate affair.

To mitigate these challenges, your best bet is to communicate clearly and promptly with your teams. Put systems in place to ensure that you can always reach all members of your staff, even if they are off work. This is important because companies operate in an environment that is currently unpredictable and depends on the decisions of local, state, and federal governments, which the company has no control over. Therefore, if any of these change agents make a decision that affects work in one way or the other, like imposing a lockdown, you should be able to reach all your employees with information on the way forward.

This is also the best time to decentralize decision making. Encourage team managers to take active roles and be more proactive on matters concerning their teams. Until everything is streamlined, it will be much easier to manage teams in this manner than waiting until all pandemic-related changes are implemented.

2. Fostering Trust

Remote working is the in-thing in the corporate workspace. However, this move wasn't voluntary for many companies. Remote working was a matter of necessity and resulted in unexpected cultural changes.

When you have wholesale changes taking place at the same time, there are bound to be trust issues across different factions of the business. You can address these by encouraging managers and team leaders to hold daily briefings where they highlight their plans and encourage their team members to speak freely about pain points or any other challenges that might affect their delivery. Honest communication is vital in these briefings so that it's easier to offer support when employees raise concerns.

3. Prompt Communication

One thing that has been evident throughout the pandemic is that arising issues are usually tackled on a case-by-case basis. For this reason, it's important to communicate with your teams regularly to make sure they are always informed on progress or changes in the company that affect their mandate.

At a personal level, employees also have to keep up with instructions from governments and other agencies to keep them safe. Usually, once the government makes an announcement, a sense of panic and confusion ensues as every entity tries to make sense of the announcements and interpret them with respect to their industry. This is where the role of HR comes in. You must communicate and offer clarity to your employees as soon as the government takes a stand on issues affecting your business.

For example, if the government announces a nationwide vaccination drive, you should pick up on that and update your employees on how this will affect them, what you expect of them, and other useful resources that can help them. If there's anything you can do to further simplify the process for them, let them know, and encourage them to get in touch for further support or clarification as needed.

The point of prompt communication is to eliminate ambiguities. The pandemic, vaccines, and relevant containment measures have largely been divisive subjects, and since everyone is entitled to their opinions and decisions affecting their families, the most you can do is not to impose but to review government instructions and give your team a clear sense of direction on compliance.

Perhaps one of the most important things you can communicate to your employees during such times is offering them assurances that their positions are safe and, regardless of the situation, the company will always do everything possible to protect them.

Chapter 9

Covid-19-Specific Paid Sick Leave and Accommodations

How do you handle COVID-19 cases?

One thing about the virus is that while most symptoms cut across the board, the severity might vary from one person to the next. This is also in line with the possibility of underlying medical conditions that the affected individual might have. How do you accommodate the needs of your affected employees since each infection comes with varied effects?

As businesses start reopening, HR needs to come up with a clear plan of action to handle any eventualities. The good news for employees is that there are specific laws that offer protections for persons who are affected by the virus and offer the necessary accommodations to them.

In terms of accommodations, the company must ensure that employees have all the necessary resources unless they would be too difficult for the employer to reasonably provide. Exceptions to this also include situations where providing the accommodations needed would put the safety and health of other employees at risk or alter the nature of the employee's job significantly.

Some of the accommodations available to employees during this period include working from home where possible, reassignment, or restructuring the job in a manner that allows the employee to keep delivering on their mandate. Remote working has largely been a success throughout the global workforce, so on that front, it's safe to admit that employers have done reasonably well so far.

The need for job restructuring arises where the employer must make certain adjustments or changes to make it feasible to perform your job roles. To this end, it might be sensible for the employer to restructure your work in a way that doesn't warrant interacting with other team members or customers directly. Since the pandemic started, we've seen many companies switch to online payment platforms instead of handling cash deposits. This makes the work environment safer for both the employees and customers.

Where necessary, employers might also opt to reassign some employees. This is simply being assigned a different role. The reason for reassignment is also similar to restructuring; it's to ensure that employees don't spend more time around customers or their workmates. This is meant to reduce exposure to the virus and keep a healthy workforce. Even though working conditions might not be the same everywhere, employers are mandated to do everything possible to make the environment safe for everyone. This includes providing personal protective equipment (PPE) for employees to use within the relevant confines, like gloves or masks, or offering paid sick leave to the affected employees.

The accommodations discussed above are things that are widely accepted as legal requirements that all employers must meet. However, this doesn't stop an employer from offering other accommodations that might not be expressly prescribed within the legal framework of their jurisdiction. At the company level, it's advisable to discuss possible accommodations with your employees depending on the nature of your operation and how their work is affected by the disruptions from the pandemic.

The Case for Vaccination

As vaccines become widely available, employers should encourage employees to get them. This is a good initiative in that it helps to limit the risk of infection on the job, or otherwise, and might even help employers limit liability in case an employee gets infected at work. As soon as the vaccines were announced, there was widespread excitement, especially since people were tired of the doom and gloom around the pandemic. A vaccine was a sign of hope that we might get the economy reopened, lockdowns lifted, and businesses back to a point of profitability.

Obviously, vaccination is a personal choice that we must accept. It would be irresponsible for HR to victimize an employee who takes a personal stand against getting the jab. Indeed, we have other problems apart from the vaccine. For example, a lot of people simply let their guard down as soon as they get the vaccine. This is where HR must step in.

Whether employees are vaccinated or not, it's still important to stress the need for precaution. People must still exercise caution, as much as mask guidelines have been widely relaxed in many places. One thing we learned from the pandemic is that it's better to take precautions than gamble with life.

With more people expected to return to work as the vaccination drive goes on throughout the country, pegging hope on herd immunity might be futile in the long run. New infections might still be recorded and, with the risk of new mutations, this is not the time to relax the precautionary measures. We cannot afford to bring people back to work only to put them in a situation where they become more vulnerable than they were at home.

After all is said and done, employers must take a stand for the greater good of everyone, step up vaccination efforts, and encourage employees to talk about it.

One of the challenges in the uptake of vaccines within workplaces is that leaders are trying to sit on the fence, especially since the decision is a personal matter. Indeed, no organization would wish to infringe on any individual employee's rights to go for the jab or not. However, employers can provide the necessary resources and information so that people make informed decisions.

There's so many falsehoods and myths flooding social media, and unfortunately, these usually get so much more traction than the truth. The trend so far is many companies choosing not to make vaccination mandatory. While this makes sense because of the personal nature of the matter, we cannot turn a blind eye to the fact that not being vaccinated leaves an employee at risk and puts the lives of others around them at risk too.

Companies that choose flexibility and give employees full autonomy on this matter must brace themselves for the inevitable. If vaccination is not mandatory, you must then come up with elaborate work policies to protect everyone as soon as people start coming back to work. With remote working models, it might be easier for each employee to manage their health at home. If the company wishes to maintain this model permanently, whether the employee is vaccinated or not might not have much impact on the health of other employees. The only problem might be if the employee is infected and, as a result, they are unable to work.

The issue of vaccination remains a divisive matter, even though some companies resorted to incentivizing the process. On the other hand, many companies have opted to withhold any declarations until things get clearer. This explains why a lot of people are mostly still working from home and their employers have no tangible plan in place for a return-to-work formula. The companies keeping their cards close to their chests either don't have a defined plan for handling the vaccine situation or don't want to risk polarizing the workforce by taking an unpopular stand on vaccines.

We can't sit on the fence forever. At some point, even if companies opt out of making vaccines mandatory, we still have the responsibility of education. Education is the most important weapon we can use to fight the virus. This is also how to challenge and debunk common myths about the vaccine.

For those companies bold enough to take a stand on vaccination, you must also come up with policies that support employees. For example, allow them time off work to heal from possible side effects of the vaccine. Some companies even offer financial incentives to encourage uptake of the vaccine.

As we have experienced over the years with work benefits and other contentious issues, one of the most useful tools we have is effective communication. On vaccination, we cannot afford to get tired or give up along the way. Frequent, repeated communication can drive the message home.

The vaccine conversation has polarized not just employees but every other sphere of life. This makes it a difficult choice for employers, especially coming from the conversation we had in Chapter 5 about diversity and inclusion. You can work around subtle nudges so that your suggestions don't come off as mandatory impositions. One thing you can't do is take away an employee's freedom of choice.

Let's not forget that this isn't the first time companies are facing a difficult discussion on public health. Employers play an active role in several aspects of employee health, including wellness programs, flu shot fairs, health insurance, and so on. Some companies have even taken a stance on smoking or offered incentives to employees for healthy behavior. Therefore, the issue of COVID-19 vaccination should not be an exception.

Besides, the Equal Employment Opportunity Commission recently gave employers the go ahead to educate and, where necessary, incentivize vaccination drives. This is good for employers, especially those whose business models have been massively hurt by remote working. It's been more than a year of challenges and sacrifices throughout the job market, and scientists believe from research, that vaccination is the solution to rebooting the economy. This is the safest option at the moment for welcoming clients and customers back into our businesses and getting all employees back to work. This is the time for resolute leadership from employers. This is the time to rally the troops.

Legal Position on Vaccines

They might not openly admit it but many companies that are not speaking with an unwavering voice about their stand on vaccines might be playing safe to avoid legal challenges with their employees. Here are some common concerns legal teams and risk managers have to deal with:

- Can the employer legally make vaccination mandatory?

- Is the employer mandated to offer accommodations to employees who opt out of vaccination in the event that they get infected? If so, what accommodations can they offer, especially if the company has taken on a massive vaccination campaign in recent months?

- What legal reprieve does an employer have with respect to workers' compensation and any other applicable laws, assuming that an employee signs up for vaccination as instructed by the employer but then suffers adverse side effects? How much is the employer exposed in terms of potential liability claims?

- What labor protections do employees enjoy, especially if they opt out of vaccination?

- Can the employer have policies on disciplining employees who opt out of vaccination, and what are the potential legal challenges of enforcing such policies?

As different vaccines are rolled out, more employers are mulling vaccination mandates or how to implement them in the future. The prospect here is strict protocols that employees either get the vaccine or risk termination. When you have employers like Google and Goldman Sachs taking such a stand, other employers are definitely taking a closer look at unfolding events.

Understanding the ramifications of any action employers might take on vaccination means factoring in the complexities of both state and federal law alongside advice from health experts. Before you implement vaccination mandates, you should learn more about the possible consequences.

In May 2021, the Equal Employment Opportunity Commission stated that employers are not barred from asking employees to get the vaccine, citing the absence of any federal law to that effect. This means that you can go ahead and design your vaccination mandate. Employers should, however, make sure that their vaccination mandates are not meant to coerce action from employees.

The whole point of a vaccination mandate should be to protect employees and customers. Note that even though vaccination mandates are legal, you must still factor in appropriate provisions for accommodation as per the Americans with Disabilities Act (ADA) and the Civil Rights Act of 1964 (Title VII).

There are special circumstances where under federal law, you might have to offer appropriate accommodations to employees who opt out of vaccinations, citing personal beliefs, religious observance, or even disability. That being said, all issues pertaining to vaccination mandates and employee responses or reactions must be addressed in an individual capacity. This means that it is not enough to, for example, discipline an employee for failure to get vaccinated simply because you implemented a mandate to that effect. Instead, you must listen to their reasons for opting out and, from there, evaluate their request for accommodations.

In some instances, you can be guided by precedents set by state agencies. For example, state agencies cannot demand proof of vaccination as a precondition for employment, engaging the state on any business, or accessing services offered by the state. While this might be restricted to the state, you can also use this as guidance in case you don't have any iron-clad policies of your own yet.

On the same note, there isn't much legal closure on whether employers have the mandate to demand vaccination status from employees or potential hires. This means that employers can request this information without contravening any prohibitions as outlined by the ADA on inquiries about disabilities. That being said, there's a limit to the kind of questions an employer can ask. For example, while the employer can ask whether an employee is vaccinated or not, follow-up questions on the employee's reasons, beliefs, or motivations for not taking the vaccination or the manner in which they are asked, might be violations as per federal law. Therefore, as an employer, you must exercise caution when engaging employees and not ask more questions than you need to. You might also be in violation of federal law if you store that information.

Additionally, you must also understand the different legal privileges that employees enjoy. For example, most employees might be concerned that asking for their vaccinations status is a violation of their rights under the Health Insurance Portability and Accountability Act (HIPAA). The protections under this act do not apply to employers, but only to health plans, health care providers, and clearinghouses. In some cases, it might also affect any business partners affiliated with the said entities.

In cases where the employer offers an incentive to get more employees vaccinated, it's only natural that the employer would wish to see proof of vaccination before granting the incentive. In such instances, the employer's request for proof of vaccination does not constitute a breach of legal statutes.

Before implementing a vaccination mandate, you should be careful not to overstep your legal boundaries. This is because there are so many practical and legal considerations that govern vaccination mandates in the workplace. If you are ever uncertain, consult your risk and compliance teams and attorneys on the best way forward.

Chapter 10

HR Teams and Marijuana Usage Laws

Marijuana usage has always been a thorny subject, even before the pandemic. More people admittedly use recreational marijuana since the pandemic, buoyed by the fact that more states have since legalized its use. For employers, this means a high chance that more employees will test positive for marijuana if, or when, a drug test is administered. The challenge for HR is not only on the legal status of marijuana but also the contentious issue of employee rights.

According to Quest Diagnostics, one of the major drug testing labs contracted by companies in the US, more employees tested positive for marijuana during the pandemic than the period before the pandemic (Quest Diagnostics, 2021). The pandemic has been a troubling experience for many people, and it is understandable that many would resort to the use of marijuana for different reasons, especially to manage anxiety.

While widespread legalization of marijuana is welcome for various reasons, the challenge for HR is how to refine and update drug policies without infringing on employees' rights to privacy, especially at a time when most people are working from home. At the time of this publication, marijuana was still illegal under federal law. However, developments around the Cannabis Administration and Opportunity Act might change the landscape in the future (Booker et al., 2021).

On the above grounds, the illegality of marijuana under federal law, coupled with the state-specific legalization, means that employers still reserve the right to test employees for marijuana. Under specific circumstances, employers can also, within the confines of their drug policies, discipline employees who test positive. Until there are conclusive reports on the federal position of marijuana, everything around it will always be addressed on a case-by-case basis. There are many gray areas, particularly when addressing medicinal marijuana.

At the community level, marijuana has enjoyed widespread acceptance since the 2018 Farm Bill: the first time federal legislation delisted hemp as a schedule 1 controlled substance according to the Drug Enforcement Administration (DEA). As a result, the use of cannabidiol (CBD) has increased over the years, especially in the wellness industry. Responding to the hype, some employers have since taken a softer stand on the matter in their policies.

A trend is emerging, perhaps in anticipation of further developments on the matter, where some employers have removed marijuana from the list of drugs that could warrant disciplinary action, while others have only stopped screening for tetrahydrocannabinol (THC), the active ingredient in marijuana.

While still grappling with the uncertainties around marijuana, COVID-19 pretty much threw a spanner in the works. For fear of exposure, many employees and job candidates feel uncomfortable visiting a clinic for drug testing thereby leaving employers in a tight spot. As mentioned earlier, many people have understandably resorted to the use of marijuana as a stress reliever and to manage anxiety occasioned by the pandemic. How does HR approach this? Is drug testing still a priority, and with people working from their homes, at what point does HR's agenda breach the employee's privacy?

Communication is Key

Admittedly, pandemic or no pandemic, drug testing is in the employer's best interest and, to a larger extent, that of the entire workforce. Picture a situation where the overall performance of a team is affected by the erratic behavior of one or a few members on some substance. In the large scheme of things, anything that is detrimental to performance might have a similar impact on compensation or remuneration. There are so many reasons why drug testing remains a priority, and the benefits to employers and employees have also been widely documented over the years. This, therefore, is not in dispute.

Amidst the uncertainties around marijuana and the pandemic, HR can step in and bridge the gap through effective communication. Before you send job applicants or your employees to your preferred testing centers, pass the information to them. Since drug testing is a standard policy in most organizations, consider revising the policy to highlight the need for social distancing, wearing masks, and other COVID-19 prevention measures. Your employees' well-being and safety are just as important as the need for drug testing.

As you review the policies, be clear on the definition or the acceptable limits of the workplace. The workplace should be any location where the employee performs some work for the employer. This might mean that even in your home, as long as you are working on something for your employer, that space becomes a workplace and a drug-free zone as per company policies.

Once you make this clear, you should also follow through and share written policy updates with your employees. With this communication, you can then encourage and train team leaders, supervisors, and managers on how to detect erratic behavior or impairment during their interactions with employees, prompting further action.

Note that communicating policies to your team might still not get you out of the woods yet. What happens if an employee is adamant they will not get tested? Well, the first thing that anyone would suggest is disciplinary action because testing is mandatory. While this might be true, it might not always be a safe bet. Instead of jumping to disciplinary action, find out the individual's reason for refusal. Perhaps the employee has an underlying medical condition, hence the refusal. Therefore, effective communication will go a long way in making things easier and avoiding unnecessary legal action.

Should HR Be Concerned?

When it comes to marijuana, there's never a straight answer. In your oversight role as HR, however, you need to be clear on company policy. Boredom, the rigors of social isolation, anxiety, stress, and routine changes are commonly fronted as reasons for the increased use of marijuana in light of the pandemic. Despite this knowledge, however, you cannot ignore the fact that the consumption patterns necessitated by the factors above could easily result in dependence problems.

The reasons for use notwithstanding, it would be irresponsible to ignore the potential long-term challenges of using marijuana. Therefore, even in instances where your company and state allow the use of marijuana, you must still be keen on usage patterns so that you can preempt problematic consequences and suggest useful resources to the affected employees.

Short-term effects of using marijuana might include impaired control, physical coordination, and cognitive function. This leaves the user vulnerable to injury or accidents. With more states legalizing marijuana, these are valid concerns that employers must contend with going forward. Your company policies and actions must take into consideration the existing marijuana laws in your state. Take the case of Arizona as an example, which allows the use of marijuana to treat or manage medical conditions.

In this regard, your drug use policies must be clear and concise in terms of your expectations of employees, especially if recreational marijuana is legalized in your state. This is particularly important if testing positive for marijuana results in disciplinary action in your organization. Without clear policies and communication with your employees, you might end up in a situation where people use marijuana since it is legal within your state and, thus, feel discriminated against when summoned for disciplinary action.

Eventually, you need to decide whether you'll maintain the same drug testing policies as before the pandemic or not, especially if you operate in a state where recreational marijuana is legal. This applies particularly to pre-hiring tests. Your current employees might understand your policies and abide by them but potential hires might not. The last thing you want is to be labeled a discriminatory employer by jobseekers.

At some point, you might have to make a judgment call on marijuana testing, especially in states where marijuana is widely accepted. For example, if an employee's use of marijuana away from the confines of your work does not interfere with their performance, you really don't need to be concerned, right? So eventually, the ultimate decision might come down to the employee's reaction and response. If their performance is affected, or if they become a safety risk after using marijuana, then at that point you must put your foot down and lay down the law. Remember, however, that the only way you can affect this is through clear communication of your company policies on drug use and testing. On marijuana use, leave nothing to chance.

Future Outlook

There was a massive drop in the number of drug tests occasioned by employers during the pandemic. This coincides with the fact that fewer companies were requesting drug tests, signaling an increase in unemployment. On the other hand, more people were self-medicating through the pandemic, which resulted in a higher number of positive drug tests than before. It's not just the use of marijuana but the consumption of alcohol also went up, alongside reported drug overdoses.

Marijuana usage was already on the rise before the pandemic. The pandemic only accelerated the phenomenon. In the push to resume work, millions of people will be trying to join or rejoin the workforce, and a good number will probably test positive for some substance, particularly marijuana and alcohol. With this in mind, there's widespread concern among HR circles about the future of the employment scene.

Certainly, drug testing is not going away. People might have concerns about some facilities but, from a professional point of view, you cannot let your guard down on drug testing. Indeed, the industry has evolved and, with it, we now have more effective and sophisticated testing technology to work with. Hair testing, oral fluid, and urine testing still provide accurate and legal results, so we can expect this to go on into the future.

Employers must rise to different challenges occasioned by the pandemic. For example, many clinics struggled with urine sample collections because they were overwhelmed by COVID-19 cases. As a result, you might have to consider other forms of testing like saliva screening or oral fluid drug testing. Oral fluid testing, for example, is a simple, yet effective, process that can be administered either with a trained expert or by employees within your work premises. It also eliminates the need to visit clinics and other facilities.

Where possible, urine testing is still the most ideal procedure. With a detection period of up to four days, this test can easily identify a wide range of drugs and substances. If your state legalized marijuana, oral fluid testing is a good option because substances can be identified within minutes of use. The fact that it can deliver results in hours makes it a reliable tool for detecting recent substance use compared to other methods. Finally, hair testing is perfect for proving historical drug use since the window of detection is up to three months but would be futile if you needed to detect recent use.

The methods outlined above are practical, accurate, and legally acceptable. Their detection periods will determine which one to implement, depending on the kind of result you seek. Practically, however, using a combination of two or all three where possible should deliver the best results and returns on your drug testing program.

Whichever of the three options you choose, you might also have to review your collections policy for drug tests. Granted, many people feel uncomfortable walking into a drug testing facility or a clinic if they are not sick, for fear of contracting COVID-19. As much as drug testing is a mandatory exercise, you should make it as comfortable and convenient as possible for your team. Where possible, allow your employees to provide samples either at work or at home. Several telehealth and video-observed collection methods are available to safeguard the integrity of this process.

As you review your alcohol and drug testing policies going forward, consistency and uniformity will help you get your employees to appreciate the processes. Any changes to the drug testing policy should be widely reviewed by your legal and risk management teams to make sure that your policies do not contravene federal, state, or local testing requirements.

Ultimately, remind everyone that drug testing is primarily aimed at offering a safe and conducive business environment for everyone. The process might be more challenging because of the pandemic but it is still important nonetheless.

Chapter 11

Supporting Mental Health

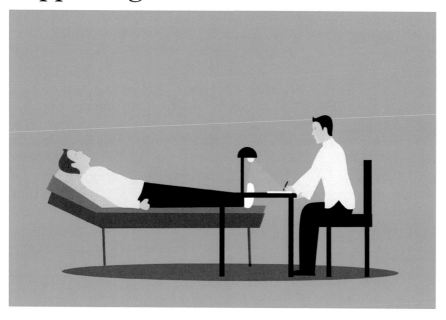

Mental health is an important part of our well-being. Like physical health, it exists along a spectrum. We all operate between good physical health and having critical or even fatal health problems, and the same can be said of mental health. Given that there are many factors responsible for your present mental state, you can end up on whichever side of the spectrum in an instant.

Stress is one of the key factors that determines most people's mental state. As there are many stressors in your immediate environment, it's always important to try and understand their impact and learn how to mitigate the unpleasant effects. In modern society, the work environment plays a big role in the mental health of employees.

The interesting thing about the work environment is that the relationship to mental health isn't restricted to the workplace. Other factors like the environment at home and everything else that takes place between the home and work can also affect someone's mental health. For example, some people find an enabling and supportive workplace a good escape from unstable homes, while others can't wait for the workday to end so they can escape the toxic environment.

Given that there are many factors that come into play when discussing mental health at work, HR teams have always had a difficult time addressing this issue. The fact that some HR leaders might not have experience with psychological training further makes it a difficult concept to address with defined precision. The most you can do is address work-related issues that might influence employee well-being.

Anxiety, stress, and terrible moods are common indicators that an employee might not be in the right frame of mind. Obsessive-compulsive disorders (OCD), phobias, anxiety, and depression are common mental health challenges that you can come across in a diverse workforce. Since the pandemic had many people working from home, it's been difficult to address these issues because most of the time HR doesn't get to interact with employees on a face-to-face basis.

While remote working has been great for employees who struggled with toxic work environments, it also made it difficult for employees who found solace in each other's company, sharing ideas, and opening up about their personal challenges. That's without looking at the unique personal challenges that people faced directly as a result of the pandemic, either within their households, families, or communities.

The role of HR in these trying times is to do everything within their mandate to ensure that employee mental health and well-being take precedence. The COVID-19 situation keeps changing from time to time, even with access to different vaccines. One thing that's guaranteed is that employees will keep feeling the changing impact of the pandemic from time to time. To address these challenges, HR must pay more attention to behavioral patterns, health, and changes. Gone are the days when HR would recommend resources and references to employees who had mental health challenges. HR must now be proactive and follow up to see whether the resources were useful or not.

The pandemic didn't just disrupt the normal workflow. It also disrupted home setups and social interactions, which are important in establishing a healthy work-life balance. This means that more employees are feeling the pinch and pandemic-related trauma is on the rise. With increasing stress levels, HR faces an uphill task in terms of managing employee resilience.

HR must, therefore, shift their attention to employee support services. If some large employers who probably had mental health support systems in place before the pandemic are struggling, the plight of relatively smaller employers could be worse.

Even though mental health is often a stigmatized subject in many workplaces, HR must champion and create the right environment for open conversations around the subject at all levels of the organization. To achieve this, HR must embrace flexibility and transparency in addressing the needs of employees. Alongside the organizations' performance and workflow needs, employers must also take employee mental and behavioral health seriously.

The Challenge Ahead

Self-isolation, travel restrictions, and other measures introduced during the pandemic created a lot of challenges. Other than the fear of contracting the virus, many people struggled with anxiety as a result of the experiences of their friends, family members, and close associates. Many lost loved ones and couldn't attend funerals or condole with their loved ones. By the time we resume normal working conditions, the reality of empty spaces, missing colleagues will come down hard on a lot of people. It will never be business as usual.

Even before the pandemic, job security was a common concern in every other industry. Now more than ever, it is an obvious concern.

The fear of navigating the unknown without the comfort of a regular salary has many people worried, further contributing to the challenge of anxiety and other mental health problems that might already plague the working class. Combining family and work commitments means that some people are working longer or more irregular hours than they did before the pandemic, which only makes already strained attempts at work-life balance worse.

Isolation, reduced motivation, absence of purpose, increased use of alcohol and drugs, fatigue, and limited exercise are some of the common health challenges that many people have been facing during the pandemic. Learning from other pandemics prior, the effects of these challenges are long-term, which means that we are looking at a future where more people might struggle with PTSD, depression, anger, stress, and irritability.

It's fair to admit that many employers went out of their way to make life relatively easier for their teams by addressing mental health concerns affecting their teams. HR must build on this and plan for long-term mental health concerns to mitigate the challenges ahead. We must also tackle the misconception that once we achieve the desired levels of vaccination and other measures to combat the virus, life will reset and go back to normal. This will not happen, at least not in the near future.

For all the strides humanity has made in dealing with the pandemic, the biggest challenge lies in trying to restore normalcy. Everyone suffered from or was affected by the pandemic in a different manner. For those who had first-hand experience with the virus, the paranoia might not go away anytime soon. Some people are scarred for life.

One of the challenges facing employers post-pandemic is that people's expectations and needs have changed and will continue to do so for a long time. An inclusive work environment or culture has to involve more than free drinks every weekend or any other privileges they enjoy on the company's tab. Going forward, you must be authentic in your attempts to support employees. People need tangible support, especially on mental health matters.

The challenge for many employers will be how to incorporate mental health in their work culture, especially in workplaces where the subject is largely stigmatized. To be effective, this should be an evolving exercise with input from employees. For example, find out what they feel about the company's current policies or programs on mental health. What do they think is missing? What opportunities exist that haven't been tapped yet? How can you help them feel better about working for the company during and after the pandemic?

Next, you'll have to think about budgeting. Effective mental health support programs shouldn't be resource intensive. HR should come up with a cost-effective plan that addresses the team's needs. If you come up with a plan that's breaking your budget, then you're probably not doing it right.

Look at it this way, mental health is a part of who we are. Mental health is every day. Start by vouching for a commitment from the top brass in the company. The idea here is not just to inform employees, but to show them that the organization is fully committed to prioritizing their mental health. If they need someone to talk to, they'll have it. If someone needs a few days away, it can be arranged. They need to understand that there's always someone they can speak to.

Depending on the structure of your company, you might have to liaise with local mental health agents to offer safe and comfortable spaces for your team. This can also be a good opportunity to tap into existing skills and talents within the team. For example, some of your employees might be life coaches, yoga instructors, or counselors. Bring them on board and discuss how they can leverage their skills to help the company improve the overall work experience. Such initiatives can also help to reignite a sense of togetherness in the workplace, especially at a time when many people have retreated to their individual cocoons in light of the pandemic.

Finally, you must create a sense of acceptance. Help your team understand that it is perfectly okay and normal to not feel okay. This is particularly an important statement that applies to you. Whether you are the only HR manager or in charge of a team, your mental health is equally important. It can be mentally taxing to steer your workforce through a pandemic if you can't take care of your mental health. Take some of the advice you dish out and cut yourself some slack. You too, need to be cared for.

Early Intervention Measures

It's always easier to respond to and handle mental health problems if you can identify the signs and symptoms early enough. This is only possible if they are clearly articulated throughout the company. Early intervention measures can effectively help you prevent the situation from getting worse. Remember that mental health is not just the preserve of management but impacts the entire workforce. To this end, make it easier for everyone to access any mental health information and support resources necessary. This makes it easier for fellow employees to recognize behavioral changes, early patterns, and signs that might prompt them to ask for help or suggest it to management.

Note that with the remote working models it might be difficult to identify some of the common mental health symptoms, so creating a system where employees check in frequently and interact with one another online can bridge this gap. Some of the signs you should discuss include withdrawal symptoms, aggression, anger, irritability, sudden mood changes, working too long without breaks, anti-social behavior, confusion, indecision, distraction, sudden lateness, and overreacting to issues or problems.

Remember that the occurrence of one or more of these symptoms isn't necessarily a sign of mental health problems. However, a pattern of occurrence might be worth looking into. As much as it is encouraging to have an open discussion with an employee about their mental health and share your concern, be careful not to project assumptions as this might make them apprehensive.

Check in with the affected individual from time to time; call in and have a casual conversation about how they are doing. If you notice a pattern of concerning changes, address them in a non-judgmental manner, and ask the employee if they need any assistance or if they have suggestions on how you can ease their burden.

These conversations might not necessarily have to involve HR. If you have an elaborate management system in place, your managers and supervisors might take the hot seat on this one. Talk to them about how to handle these conversations so that they can support their team members without being intrusive. Discuss how to identify instances where an employee might need professional help and how to bring it up.

Of course, whether phased or not, we will all return to work at some point. Start making advanced plans on how to streamline this experience. After more than a year working from home, anticipate a lot of friction when people start working from the offices. Don't wait for the entire team to return to work and deal with the challenges. Discuss them right now. Find out how they feel about returning to work, given their experiences from working remotely. What are their fears and concerns? How have their living arrangements been affected? Perhaps they are now primary caregivers for vulnerable family members. All these dynamics affect their mental health and should be factored into any plans for a phased return-to-work program.

Finally, you need to communicate details of the company's return-to-work plans. Show your employees that the plans notwithstanding their safety and mental health are a top priority, and the company will provide all the support they need.

Practical Solutions to Tackling Mental Health

As the uncertainty around the pandemic keeps unfolding, one thing remains unchanged —the role of the manager. Traditionally, your role, whether in HR or whichever other department, is to provide all the support your team needs to deliver on their job description. With the pandemic, this largely involves caring for their mental health. Many HR managers who haven't been in a position to deal with mental health concerns with the severity prompted by the pandemic might be unsure of how to go about this. Interestingly, most of the mental health support services, skills, and resources your team might require are pretty much the same ones you need to become an effective and reliable leader. Let's discuss some practical solutions below that you can implement in your organization right away:

Practice Vulnerability

Perhaps one of the unexpected benefits of the pandemic is that while it resulted in many people struggling with mental health, it also pushed corporate society into openly talking about the subject. Mental health has not been one of the easiest discussions in corporate society for a long time, with many people shying away from the topic for fear of coming off as weak or unfit for the cut-throat nature of their industries.

It's fair to say that most people endured some level of discomfort and mental strain, and with that in mind, we can hope for less stigma around mental health. Going forward, you can build on this in your capacity and encourage people to be honest about their mental health. Of course, you can anticipate some apprehension along the way, but by creating safe spaces for your employees to express their concerns, you lay the foundation for a successful approach to addressing mental health now, and in the future, if people ever return to work fully.

The whole point of vulnerability, especially when championed by management, is to remind and show everyone else that you are just as human as they are. Whether your pets or kids crash your meeting or your partner absentmindedly disrupts with a quirky remark, putting these simple things out there helps your employees relate better. They understand that you are going through the same challenges they do. At some point, you might even joke about them. Such interactions can boost performance, engagement, and more importantly, trust within your workforce.

Lead by Example

In many organizations, support for mental health is usually implied. HR has to do more than that and actually show that you support mental health. Provide tangible solutions that show your employees that their mental health is a priority. With people working remotely, encourage them to take time off work and do something relaxing, like relaxing in their backyard, taking a walk, or playing with their kids.

The idea here is to shift the focus from work to their overall well-being by encouraging them to be more aware of their surroundings and to enjoy themselves while at it. Remind them that work can, and should be fun, especially now that they are working from home in an environment where they have complete control.

It's easier to pass this message along if they can see you doing it. For example, let them know you have an appointment with your therapist to clear your head during this difficult time. This makes the mental health discussion and asking for help relatable. Encourage them to take one or two hours and turn off all work-related stuff, like emails or the work phone. Some employees feel guilty doing some of these things, so your task is to show them it's a normal thing and that they are more valuable to the company if they are in the right frame of mind.

Mental Health Training

This is the best time for your company to invest in preventive mental health training. Everyone including management and supervisors will benefit from these lessons and help you create a healthy mental culture in your organization.

Many uncertainties have come up since the pandemic, and learning how to address them can help you fight stigma at work and debunk mental health myths at all levels. If your company cannot afford this, you can always reach out to local mental health support networks for support.

You have a responsibility to your employees to create an environment that is conducive to their mental health and well-being in general. Go beyond the regular check-in questions and find out how they are doing. With more people working remotely, it's getting harder for HR to keep up and tell whether employees are okay or not. The only way you can overcome these challenges is to establish a culture of listening to their concerns, quality connections, and offering inclusive and flexible solutions to their challenges, both in the office and in their remote working spaces.

As much as we hold onto hope that normalcy will resume and life goes on as it was in 2019, this will not happen, at least not in the near future. The lessons learned from the pandemic offer great opportunities to establish healthy behavioral change patterns at work that will not just help those who are returning to work but should have actually been in place years before the pandemic.

Conclusion

The majority of the working population haven't been to their offices in more than a year. That's the impact of COVID-19. However, even before the pandemic, many companies were already exploring the possibility of remote working schedules, so this isn't a new thing. What's new is the disruption in schedules and work routines, which might persist for a while longer than we can anticipate. As much as there's more research and progress in understanding the virus today, there's no guarantee that we'll be out of the woods anytime soon. The best we can do is hope for the best but brace ourselves for the worst.

One of the best traits of humanity is our resilience in the face of adversity and the ability to adapt to new realities. Switching from the traditional workplace environment to a virtual experience is fast becoming the new reality in many companies. Instead of working alongside colleagues, people are now working alongside relatives, toddlers, roommates, pets, or even out in the woods surrounded by birds and other elements of nature. This is the new normal and, for HR managers, it creates as many challenges as it offers solutions to real-time post-pandemic problems.

Regardless of the progress made from remote working, the fact is that at some point, people will have to return to their offices. The reality is that many people have enjoyed remote working, and they have found it more peaceful and productive, working in an environment where they have full control over most elements they normally wouldn't in the workplace.

Companies are also evolving, and we can expect some transformative changes in the work environment after the pandemic. The idea is to rethink the workplace dynamics to meet the emerging needs and demands of employers and employees. The role of HR management is to champion this dynamic and be the change driver to ensure a seamless transition back to work, where applicable.

The dynamic changes in the workplace environment are not limited to rethinking physical working needs. A big chunk of changes involve managing skills, abilities, and the needs of employees in line with the nature and demand for work after the pandemic.

It's not all doom and gloom though. One positive take away from the pandemic is the concern for employee well-being. This is something that many organizations had struggled with before the pandemic but has since taken center stage, and generally, HR teams have become more aware of the general well-being of their employees. This trend will help to bridge the gap between efficient delivery and helping employees own their input and realizing that their health and overall well-being are important to the organization.

The rigors of a global workforce might exert a toll on HR teams, especially for companies with employees spread across the world. Naturally, there will be as many challenges as there are opportunities as people try to blend in and find their balance in the new normal. With this in mind, it's imperative that HR managers find ways of allocating resources to talent acquisition and allocation not just across departments but also across borders. Depending on the size and nature of your operation, HR managers might soon come from managing an entire office to managing an entire team spread all over the country or across the world. Without close physical supervision, HR managers might struggle to present the organization's vision, mission, and brand identity in unison, considering the multicultural aspects of diversely remote workplaces.

Many employees breathed a sigh of relief when they had to relocate from the expensive cities hosting their companies to rural areas or affordable towns. For some people, it made economic sense to relocate from the country altogether. Practically, as long as you can work from anywhere in the world and still deliver as per your job description, all you need is an internet connection. While this has largely worked for many employees, HR managers must find ways of handling this transition effectively. Transition management has always posed a challenge to many organizations, even before the pandemic. Think about the culture, mindset, capability, and abilities of employees to adapt to the ever-changing business environment. This might continue after the pandemic, with both the employees and the organization facing a host of personal or industry-specific constraints.

One area where HR managers will need to pay more attention is talent management. This is because of the need to manage the new dynamics of collaboration across projects. With more people working from home, the conventional office rapport will wane over time. Most people whose lives revolve around workplace interactions and relationships might struggle with personal connections away from the office in light of remote working models. Thus, HR must find ways of helping people engage and foster stronger relationships.

To achieve this, hybrid work schedules might come in handy: a careful blend of working from home and office attendance. This might involve organizing sessions like retreats for the team to brainstorm and bond while adhering to the relevant safety guidelines. More importantly, HR should also encourage employees to share their experiences on remote work and coping with the pandemic during these sessions. This can make it easier for more people to open up and see their personal challenges from a different perspective.

The reality of life after the pandemic is that HR managers and teams must adapt and evolve with the changing times. Any organization that is unable to, or struggles to transition smoothly into the rigors of life after the pandemic, will have a hefty price to pay. This is like the beginning of the age of technology once again. Companies that did not see the need and potential of technology and thought it was just another fad paid the price. Some lagged behind as the competition outpaced them, and never caught up, while others simply disappeared into oblivion.

Until normalcy resumes, the entire workforce must be prepared to embrace new changes as they come. For HR managers, the challenge hereon is to ensure that everyone is on board. The nature of some changes might call for psychological preparedness, hence the need for HR to communicate clearly and help their teams prepare for the challenges ahead.

References

Booker, S. C., Wyden, S. R., & Schumer, S. C. (2021). *Cannabis Administration & Opportunity Act.* https://www.democrats.senate.gov/imo/media/doc/CAOA%20Detailed%20Summary%20-.pdf

Burden, L., & Clarey, K. (2020, August 5). *As HR pursues agility, lack of strategy stands in its way, Gartner finds.* HR Dive. https://www.hrdive.com/news/as-hr-pursues-agility-lack-of-strategy-stands-in-its-way-gartner-finds/582763/

Burt, E. (2019). *Nudge theory can help change your employees' behaviour (without them even realising).* People Management. https://www.peoplemanagement.co.uk/long-reads/articles/nudge-theory-change-employees-behaviour-without-realising

Case, T. (2021, March 8). *The pandemic has bosses and employees craving the benefits of cannabis.* Digiday. https://digiday.com/future-of-work/cannabis-and-the-workplace-the-pandemic-has-bosses-and-employees-craving-its-benefits/

CIPD. (2021). *Coronavirus (COVID-19): Mental health support for employees.* CIPD. https://www.cipd.co.uk/knowledge/culture/well-being/supporting-mental-health-workplace-return

Douglas, E. (2021, September 6). *There's a mental health pandemic coming – here's how to prepare.* Hcamag.com; HRD Canada. https://www.hcamag.com/ca/news/general/theres-a-mental-health-pandemic-coming-heres-how-to-prepare/309000

Ferri, R. (2020). *People analytics: Planning for post-COVID-19 success.* GR8 People. https://www.gr8people.com/blog/talent-acquisition/people-analytics-how-to-plan-for-success-in-a-post-coronavirus-world

Ford, N. (2021). *Creating a safe work environment for a return to business during pandemic response.* Skillsoft. https://www.skillsoft.com/blog/creating-a-safe-work-environment-for-a-return-to-business-during-pandemic-response

Gautam, A. (2019, June 17). *The importance of agility in human resources.* Training Industry. https://trainingindustry.com/articles/strategy-alignment-and-planning/the-importance-of-agility-in-human-resources/

Georgetown SCS. (2021, May 17). *5 HR trends for the post-pandemic workplace.* Georgetown.edu; Georgetown University School of Continuing Studies. https://scs.georgetown.edu/news-and-events/article/8419/5-hr-trends-for-post-pandemic-workplace

Ghosh, P. (2021, March 3). *What is people analytics? Definition, process, trends, and tools.* Toolbox. https://www.toolbox.com/hr/hr-analytics/articles/what-is-people-analytics/

Goodwin, B. (2021, January 22). *Council post: Mental health during the pandemic and its impact on the workplace.* Forbes. https://www.forbes.com/sites/forbesbusinesscouncil/2021/01/25/mental-health-during-the-pandemic-and-its-impact-on-the-workplace/?sh=5ffb8eb52422

Gothelf, J. (2017, June 19). *How HR can become agile (and why it needs to).* Harvard Business Review. https://hbr.org/2017/06/how-hr-can-become-agile-and-why-it-needs-to

Greenwood, K., & Krol, N. (2020, August 7). *8 ways managers can support employees' mental health.* Harvard Business Review. https://hbr.org/2020/08/8-ways-managers-can-support-employees-mental-health

Gregory, R. (2021, May 25). *The power of nudge: How behavioural science and AI can improve workplace wellbeing.* Workplace Insight. https://workplaceinsight.net/the-power-of-nudge-how-behavioural-science-and-ai-can-improve-workplace-wellbeing/

Griffin, S. (2020, November 25). *The importance of business agility in the new normal.* Corporate Vision Magazine. https://www.corporatevision-news.com/the-importance-of-business-agility-in-the-new-normal/

Hancock, B., & Schaninger, B. (2021, May 20). *How HR chiefs can help their organizations thrive in the post-pandemic future.* Fortune. https://fortune.com/2021/05/20/human-resources-hr-training-compensation-post-pandemic-strategy-business-after-covid/

Hirsch, A. S. (2021, May 11). *Supporting mental health in the post-pandemic workplace.* SHRM. https://www.shrm.org/resourcesandtools/hr-topics/employee-relations/pages/supporting-mental-health-in-the-post-pandemic-workplace.aspx

Khan, T., Komm, A., Maor, D., & Pollner, F. (2021, June 4). *"Back to human": Why HR leaders want to focus on people again.* McKinsey & Company. https://www.mckinsey.com/business-functions/organization/our-insights/back-to-human-why-hr-leaders-want-to-focus-on-people-again

Lewis, N. (2020, April 22). *HR Managers Rethink Their Role During the Coronavirus Pandemic.* SHRM. https://www.shrm.org/hr-today/news/hr-news/pages/hr-managers-rethink-their-work-coronavirus-pandemic.aspx

Mayer, K. (2021, July 21). *How HR leaders can stay ahead on mental health support for workers.* HRExecutive.com. https://hrexecutive.com/how-hr-leaders-can-stay-ahead-on-mental-health-support-for-workers/

Ponnappa, S. (2021, June 19). *HR management in a post-pandemic world: How processes and technology will evolve.* People Matters. https://www.peoplemattersglobal.com/article/strategic-hr/hr-management-in-a-post-pandemic-world-how-processes-and-technology-will-evolve-29725?media_type=article&subcat=hr-

technology&title=hr-management-in-a-post-pandemic-world-how-processes-and-technology-will-evolve&id=29725

Quest Diagnostics. (2021). *Marijuana workforce drug test positivity continues double-digit increases to keep overall drug positivity rates at historically high levels, Finds latest Quest Diagnostics Drug Testing Index^TM analysis.* Newsroom. https://newsroom.questdiagnostics.com/2021-05-26-Marijuana-Workforce-Drug-Test-Positivity-Continues-Double-Digit-Increases-to-Keep-Overall-Drug-Positivity-Rates-at-Historically-High-Levels,-Finds-Latest-Quest-Diagnostics-Drug-Testing-Index-TM-Analysis

Routt, D. (2021, June 16). *Council post: Managing mental health in the workforce: A new role for HR professionals.* Forbes. https://www.forbes.com/sites/forbeshumanresourcescouncil/2021/06/16/managing-mental-health-in-the-workforce-a-new-role-for-hr-professionals/

Seward, Z. M. (2021, July 6). *11 important lessons about managing a hybrid workplace.* Quartz. https://qz.com/work/2028053/11-important-lessons-about-managing-a-hybrid-workplace/

Simo, Dr. T. (2021, April 8). *Marijuana + COVID-19 concerns in the workplace: How to effectively navigate drug testing.* Employment Background Check Blog - HireRight. https://www.hireright.com/blog/background-checks/marijuana-covid-19-concerns-in-the-workplace-how-to-effectively-navigate-drug-testing

Sondhi, P. (2019, May 23). *Why practicing agility matters in human resources.* Entrepreneur. https://www.entrepreneur.com/article/334180

Walsh, B. (2021, June 15). *Nudging our way to better remote work.* Axios. https://www.axios.com/humu-behavioral-science-remote-work-5ac9bfbf-1877-4434-b1a9-6e53112f05c7.html

Wilson, J. (2021, January 14). *Cannabis use rises in pandemic.* Canadian HR Reporter. https://www.hrreporter.com/focus-areas/wellness-mental-health/cannabis-use-rises-in-pandemic/336900

All images obtained from Pixabay.com

Made in United States
Orlando, FL
15 January 2023

28691253R00071